THE ESSENTIAL GUIDE TO

SPaG IN THE PRIMARY CLASSROOM

Sara Miller McCune founded SAGE Publishing in 1965 to support the dissemination of usable knowledge and educate a global community. SAGE publishes more than 1000 journals and over 800 new books each year, spanning a wide range of subject areas. Our growing selection of library products includes archives, data, case studies and video. SAGE remains majority owned by our founder and after her lifetime will become owned by a charitable trust that secures the company's continued independence.

Los Angeles | London | New Delhi | Singapore | Washington DC | Melbourne

DAVID WAUGH, KATE ALLOTT,
EVE ENGLISH, ROSEMARY WAUGH
& ELIZABETH BULMER

THE ESSENTIAL GUIDE TO
SPaG IN THE PRIMARY CLASSROOM

LM Learning Matters

Learning Matters
A SAGE Publishing Company
1 Oliver's Yard
55 City Road
London EC1Y 1SP

SAGE Publications Inc.
2455 Teller Road
Thousand Oaks, California 91320

SAGE Publications India Pvt Ltd
B 1/I 1 Mohan Cooperative Industrial Area
Mathura Road
New Delhi 110 044

SAGE Publications Asia-Pacific Pte Ltd
3 Church Street
#10-04 Samsung Hub
Singapore 049483

Editor: Amy Thornton
Senior project editor: Chris Marke
Project management: Swales & Willis Ltd, Exeter, Devon
Marketing manager: Lorna Patkai
Cover design: Wendy Scott
Typeset by: C&M Digitals (P) Ltd, Chennai, India
Printed and bound in the UK

Library of Congress Control Number: 2019948808

British Library Cataloguing in Publication Data

A catalogue record for this book is available from the British Library

ISBN 978-1-5297-1592-7
ISBN 978-1-5297-1591-0 (pbk)

At SAGE we take sustainability seriously. Most of our products are printed in the UK using responsibly sourced papers and boards. When we print overseas we ensure sustainable papers are used as measured by the PREPS grading system. We undertake an annual audit to monitor our sustainability.

CONTENTS

HOW TO USE THIS BOOK

This book is divided into 29 short chapters, each of which focuses on a key aspect of teaching and learning spelling, punctuation and grammar in schools. Chapters are divided into sections as follows.

WHAT DO I NEED TO KNOW?

This section provides you with essential knowledge about a topic to enable you to teach it with confidence.

WHAT IS IT USEFUL TO KNOW?

Here, you will find further, more detailed information that will help you deepen your understanding and deal with those challenging questions that some children ask.

KEY KNOWLEDGE SUMMARY

This short section summarises a key element of the topic concisely.

IN THE CLASSROOM

In this section, you can find out about ways in which you might plan for and teach SPaG topics in the classroom.

CLASSROOM ACTIVITIES

Chapters conclude with at least one brief lesson plan that you can use as a starting point for your planning.

Throughout the book, you will find weblinks to useful resources as well as references to further reading. You don't need to read the book from beginning to end, but we do recommend that you read Chapter 1, 'Grammar', before dipping into the book to find topics that you will be teaching. We hope that the book will show that spelling, punctuation and grammar can be interesting and engaging to teach and learn, and that a knowledge and understanding of how language works can be invaluable in developing language skills.

David Waugh

Kate Allott

Eve English

Rosemary Waugh

Elizabeth Bulmer

MEET THE AUTHORS

David Waugh is Professor of Education at Durham University where he also teaches primary English. He is a former deputy head teacher who was Head of the Education Department at the University of Hull from 2005 to 2008 and Regional Adviser for ITT for the National Strategies from 2008 to 2010. He has written and co-written or edited more than 40 books on primary education. As well as his educational writing, David also writes children's stories and regularly teaches in schools. In 2017, he wrote *The Wishroom* with 45 children from 15 East Durham schools, and recently published *Twins?* working with 12 Year 5–6 pupils.

Kate Allott is a lecturer in primary English at York St John University. She has also worked as a literacy consultant for North Yorkshire County Council, and as a regional adviser for the National Strategies Communication, Language and Literacy Development programme. Kate has written extensively on primary English and is co-author of *Language and Communication in Primary Schools* and *Primary English for Trainee Teachers*, as well as author of *Assessing Children's Writing*.

Eve English, a former head teacher, is a lecturer in English on the PGCE (Primary) and BA (QTS) courses at Durham University. She has published extensively on primary English. She is co-author of *Meeting the Standards in Primary English* and *Professional Studies in the Primary School*. Eve has a particular interest in drama and has contributed chapters on drama in *Primary English for Trainee Teachers* and *Beyond Early Writing*.

Rosemary Waugh is a linguist and former English, French, Latin and classics teacher at four schools. She has a particular interest in the history and development of grammar and etymology, and in their evolution. She is co-author of *Teaching Grammar, Punctuation and Spelling in Primary Schools* and *Children's Literature in Primary Schools*. She recently completed her first novel, *Teach Yourself Murder*.

Elizabeth Bulmer taught English literature and linguistics at various levels for several years. She took a particular interest in child language acquisition, accent and dialect, and gender differences in conversational behaviour. Sadly, Elizabeth passed away before this book was completed. Her contribution was nonetheless significant.

ACKNOWLEDGEMENTS

We are grateful to all the teachers and trainee teachers who shared their lesson ideas with us and allowed us to use them in this book.

We are also grateful to Dr Alice Earnshaw, assistant head teacher KS2 of Moorside Primary School, Lancaster, who had the original idea for creating these materials for an app and who edited the original chapters.

We would like to thank the family of the late Elizabeth Bulmer for allowing us to include the excellent materials Elizabeth created. We hope this book will remind all who knew her of Elizabeth's important contribution to education.

1

WHAT IS GRAMMAR?

WHAT DO I NEED TO KNOW?

WHY DO WE NEED TO KNOW TERMINOLOGY?

If we understand some basic terminology associated with our language, we have a shortcut for description, just as we do in other subjects such as maths. We don't have to describe the concept each time we refer to an aspect of grammar. So, for example, when teachers used to talk about using 'describing words' rather than using the term 'adjectives', they were avoiding a term that would have been easy to remember, and were also being imprecise, given that adverbs are also describing words: adjectives describe or qualify nouns, while adverbs describe or modify verbs. Thus, in the sentence below, the adjective 'dark' describes the woods, while the adverb 'slowly' tells us how Tim walked by modifying the verb.

Tim walked slowly through the dark woods.

WHAT DO WE NEED TO KNOW ABOUT GRAMMAR?

We all know lots about English grammar, even if we cannot always use terminology to describe we know what. For example, you probably noticed that the last three words of the previous sentence were in the wrong order. You may have paused and read them again, perhaps thinking there had been a misprint. Or you may have subconsciously changed the order of the words because you read quickly and expect what you read to make sense.

David Crystal (2004, pp12–13) suggests six reasons why we should learn about language:

1. 'Because it's there'. We are curious about the world and wish to understand it, and grammar is 'no different from any other domain of knowledge in this respect'.

2. Because language 'is involved with almost everything we do as human beings' and 'grammar is the fundamental organising principle of language'.

3. Because we already have an extraordinary grammatical ability and it may be helpful to describe the rules that govern grammar.

4. Because we need to be aware of what went wrong when we make grammatical errors in speech or writing.

5. Because 'learning about grammar provides a basis for learning other languages'.

6. Because after studying grammar, we should be 'more alert to the strength, flexibility and variety of our language, and thus be in a better position to use it and to evaluate others' use of it'. Crystal sounds a cautionary note here: 'Even after a course on car mechanics, we can still drive carelessly'.

The National Curriculum for English states the following:

> Throughout the programmes of study, teachers should teach pupils the vocabulary they need to discuss their reading, writing and spoken language. It is important that pupils learn the correct grammatical terms in English and that these terms are integrated within teaching.
>
> (DfE, 2013, p15)

However, a focus on grammatical terms is not exclusive to England, and an exploration of the curricula of other English-speaking countries shows that this emphasis occurs all over the world. Follow the link to the Australian National Curriculum to see how grammar is approached in another country: **www.australiancurriculum.edu.au/English/Rationale**

WHAT IS IT USEFUL TO KNOW?

GRAMMAR, SYNTAX, PUNCTUATION AND USAGE

In this section, you will discover the meanings of some of the keywords used when we discuss grammar.

GRAMMAR

Grammar refers to a set of rules about how we use language. It covers such things as how to form words, adding prefixes or suffixes to refine the meaning or to change the job a word is doing in a sentence, and how to arrange words to convey clear meaning.

SYNTAX

Syntax means the rules that define the ordering and arrangement of words within a phrase or sentence to ensure that the reader or listener understands clearly what the user meant. Syntax is a subset of grammar, and the two words are often used interchangeably.

PUNCTUATION

Punctuation is the study of the different ways in which a passage of language can be broken up into shorter units (e.g. by using commas or full stops) and the ways in which effects of speech such as surprise or doubt can be indicated in written language. Punctuation marks are the non-alphabetical symbols we use when writing, to help make meaning clear.

USAGE

Usage, as the name suggests, refers to the customary or common way that language is used, rather than to strict definitions that are sometimes out of date. We might say that 'usage is divided' over the pronunciation of the word 'economics', or that a word such as 'Eurosceptic' has 'passed into common usage'.

KEY KNOWLEDGE SUMMARY

We are all involved as teachers in the use of grammar – it is important to understand the theory and terminology of it so that we can explain what we teach and answer children's questions helpfully. Children can be helped to use language better and more creatively if they have the vocabulary to understand the process.

IN THE CLASSROOM

The English National Curriculum (DfE, 2013) sets out the grammatical terminology that pupils should know and understand:

YEAR	TERMINOLOGY FOR PUPILS
1	letter, capital letter
	word, singular, plural
	sentence
	punctuation, full stop, question mark, exclamation mark
2	noun, noun phrase
	statement, question, exclamation, command
	compound, adjective, verb, suffix
	tense (past, present)
	apostrophe, comma
3	adverb, preposition conjunction
	word family, prefix
	clause, subordinate clause
	direct speech
	consonant, consonant letter vowel, vowel letter
	inverted commas (or 'speech marks')

(Continued)

(Continued)

YEAR	TERMINOLOGY FOR PUPILS
4	determiner
	pronoun, possessive pronoun
	adverbial
5	modal verb, relative pronoun
	relative clause
	parenthesis, bracket, dash
	cohesion, ambiguity
6	subject, object
	active, passive
	synonym, antonym
	ellipsis, hyphen, colon, semicolon, bullet points

How effective is grammar teaching? Myhill et al. (2011) studied teaching strategies for developing children's writing. They found that teaching grammar as a separate topic was less effective than actively engaging children with grammar through writing. Where children learned grammar outside the context of texts, they were less likely to see its purpose.

Although the English National Curriculum has a strong emphasis upon grammar and grammatical terminology, it is interesting to note the emphasis upon learning through speaking, reading and writing:

> The grammar of our first language is learnt naturally and implicitly through interactions with other speakers and from reading. Explicit knowledge of grammar is, however, very important, as it gives us more conscious control and choice in our language. Building this knowledge is best achieved through a focus on grammar within the teaching of reading, writing and speaking. Once pupils are familiar with a grammatical concept (for example 'modal verb'), they should be encouraged to apply and explore this concept in the grammar of their own speech and writing and to note where it is used by others. Young pupils, in particular, use more complex language in speech than in writing, and teachers should build on this, aiming for a smooth transition to sophisticated writing.

(DfE, 2013, p66)

Of course, we need to remember that spoken language generally differs in some ways from written language. When we speak, we can use facial expression, voice variation and gesture to help us convey meaning. As a result, we may not need to use words and phrases that would be essential in writing.

When we speak, we also adjust our language to suit the occasion. For example, we may be more mindful of grammatical accuracy and clarity when attending an interview than when talking with our friends over a drink. This applies to writing too, and it is important that children understand that they need to vary their written style according to their audience and the text type. So, texts will differ from emails, and letters to friends will be different from formal letters.

CLASSROOM ACTIVITIES

CREATING SENTENCES USING CARDS WITH WORDS AND PUNCTUATION MARKS

RESOURCES

Make some cards with a range of common words as well as many others that are at an appropriate level for the children. Provide cards with punctuation marks and speech marks/inverted commas too. Ensure you make at least three cards with commas as these may appear more than once in a sentence.

WHAT TO DO

Ensure that each child has at least one card. Invite three children to come to the front and to hold their cards up for everyone to see. The cards might be words and/or punctuation marks. Ask the children to suggest how they might add their cards to create a sentence. For example:

The first three cards might be:

table	a	.

A child might ask to join the growing 'sentence' with the word 'big' and suggest a word order of 'a big table'.

The teacher would now need to ask the children what kind of word might be needed to help create a sentence (a verb), and another child might volunteer 'was'. Now the 'sentence' would be:

a	big	table	was	.

The children would now be asked to offer a word that might develop the 'sentence'. This could be 'set'. Although this would produce a complete sentence, the teacher can still invite the children to add to it until they are satisfied that it is as good as possible.

This activity can be developed in a variety of ways:

- More words might be added.

- Some children might be given blank cards that can act as 'jokers' (cards that can be used to represent any word the child chooses).

- The emphasis might develop into a focus on noun phrases, adverbials and fronted adverbials, adverbs, or adjectives.

- A set of pronouns can be provided so that the children can replace nouns with them.

When appropriate, teachers will use the names of word classes as sentences are constructed.

REFERENCES

Crystal, D. (2004) *Rediscover Grammar* (3rd edition). Harlow: Longman.

DfE (2013) *The National Curriculum*. London: DfE.

Myhill, D., Lines, H. and Watson, A. (2011) *Making Meaning with Grammar: A Repertoire of Possibilities*. University of Exeter, UK.

FURTHER READING

Waugh, D. and Jolliffe, W. (2017) *English 5–11: A Guide for Teachers*. London: Routledge, Chapter 5.

Waugh, D., Warner, C. and Waugh, R. (2019) *Teaching Grammar, Punctuation and Spelling in Primary Schools* (3rd edition). London: SAGE, Chapter 1.

USEFUL WEBSITE

For helpful video clips on grammar and the English National Curriculum, see **www.pearson schoolsandfecolleges.co.uk/Primary/GlobalPages/NewEnglishCurriculum/Debra-Myhill-Insights.aspx**

2

STANDARD ENGLISH

WHAT DO I NEED TO KNOW?

WHAT IS STANDARD ENGLISH?

Standard English is one dialect of English – in other words, one variety with distinctive grammatical features. It is different from other dialects because it is not linked to a geographical area. It tends to be associated with more highly educated speakers, and it is used in writing and in formal situations. As far as linguists are concerned, it is not 'better' or 'correct' when compared with other dialects, but it does typically have higher social status. It is the variety that carries most prestige in the country, and so is often recommended as a desirable educational target. Some speakers speak only Standard English (probably 10–15 per cent of the population); others switch from the dialect of their area to Standard English as appropriate to the situation. The similarities between Standard English and other dialects are many, and there are relatively few differences.

STANDARD ENGLISH AND ACCENT

Standard English has nothing to do with accent (the way words are pronounced). There is an accent known as received pronunciation (RP) that is not associated with any part of the country, as other accents are, and which tends to be used by upper- and middle-class speakers, but many Standard English speakers speak with regional accents. The opposite is not true, however; RP speakers do not use regional dialects.

FEATURES OF STANDARD ENGLISH

Standard English is not a set of rules about grammar, but it does have characteristic grammatical features that distinguish it from other dialects. Here are some examples of those features:

STANDARD ENGLISH	OTHER DIALECTS
Irregular present tense marker (i.e. I/you/we/they go, but he goes)	Other dialects tend to mark all or none (i.e. I goes, you goes, he goes, we goes, they goes, or I go, you go, he go)
No multiple negatives	Multiple negatives (e.g. I never saw nobody) – this is the opposite of French, where double negatives are the standard form and single negatives are non-standard
No distinction between second-person (you) singular and plural	Some dialects allow this distinction (e.g. you/ yous)
Irregular pronoun forms (myself, yourself, ourselves, but himself and themselves)	Pronoun forms regular (i.e. myself, yourself, hisself, theirselves)
Irregular forms of the verb 'to be', both present (I am, you are, he is, we are, you are) and past (I was, you were, he was, we were, they were)	Same form used for all persons (e.g. I be, you be, he be, we be, they be; I were, you were, he were, we were; I was, you was, we was, they was)
'This' and 'that' used to demonstrate distance from the speaker (e.g. 'not this chair, that one')	Many dialects have a three-way distinction, with 'that' meaning near the listener and 'yon' meaning far from both speaker and listener

WHY DOES STANDARD ENGLISH MATTER?

Most native speakers of English speak a non-standard form, but Standard English matters because many people need to use it in a wide range of situations. Some employers expect their employees to speak and write Standard English; as children grow older, it is increasingly expected as the form used in educational settings, and particularly in higher education. Adults who cannot switch into Standard English when appropriate may find themselves disadvantaged in a number of ways. It is therefore important that children who are not Standard English speakers at home learn to use it both in speaking and in writing.

WHAT IS IT USEFUL TO KNOW?

STANDARD ENGLISH AROUND THE WORLD

English-speaking countries around the world have their own varieties of Standard English. Australian Standard English is not exactly the same as New Zealand Standard English, for example. US Standard English differs from UK Standard English, in ways such as the US Standard English use of the verb form 'gotten'. No Standard English variety is in any way more 'correct' than any other.

LANGUAGE CHANGE AND STANDARD ENGLISH

Language changes over time, and that includes Standard English. Look at the following examples:

I was sat by the window when James came home.

I was sitting by the window when James came home.

The first has traditionally been seen as a non-standard form, with the explanation often given that it is a passive form, and therefore suggests that someone placed the speaker by the window. It is used in many dialects, along with these similar forms:

Three people were stood at the reception desk.

The couple were laid on their towels by the swimming pool.

However, the form 'was sat'/'were sat' is increasingly heard in fairly formal situations, used by educated speakers, including, a few years ago, a public-school-educated prime minister. It is therefore likely that it will, over time, come to be seen as an alternative to the traditional Standard English form.

For an account of the language change over time, see **www.bbc.co.uk/voices/yourvoice/ language_change.shtml**

STANDARD ENGLISH AND VOCABULARY

Regional dialects are characterised by vocabulary as well as grammar; they have words and expressions that are not used in other dialects (e.g. 'bairn' and 'lass' in northern dialects). This is not true of Standard English. It is true that in many more formal settings, such as lectures, business meetings, legal hearings and so on, where Standard English is used, more technical vocabulary is used, but such vocabulary is understood and used when needed by speakers of other dialects; it is not specific to Standard English.

STANDARD ENGLISH AND STYLE

Although Standard English is associated with more formal situations, and indeed is expected in them, it is also used in informal situations by some speakers, while others would switch into a regional dialect.

Consider the following examples:

I were right nithered.	Yorkshire dialect
I was frozen.	Informal Standard English
I was extremely cold.	Formal Standard English

For speakers who only speak Standard English, there is no alternative in informal situations, and they are still speaking Standard English even when they use features of informal language such as slang or fillers such as 'er', 'like', 'um' and 'I mean'.

KEY KNOWLEDGE SUMMARY

WHAT IS STANDARD ENGLISH?

Standard English is a variety of English used all over the country, in more formal situations and often by more highly educated speakers. Different varieties use slightly different grammatical forms, and regional dialects have some distinctive vocabulary.

IN THE CLASSROOM

HOW DO WE 'TEACH' STANDARD ENGLISH?

England's 2014 National Curriculum programme of study for English says that 'pupils should be taught to speak clearly and convey ideas confidently using Standard English' (DfE, 2013, p11), and the teachers' standards state that teachers must 'demonstrate an understanding of and take responsibility for promoting high standards of literacy, articulacy and the correct use of standard English' (DfE, 2012, p11).

It is therefore essential that teachers use Standard English in school. Some teachers do use a small number of regional dialect forms; they have grown up with these and are so familiar with them that they are not aware they are not standard forms. Teachers should make every effort to identify any non-standard forms they use, and then self-monitor and substitute standard forms.

IS MODELLING ENOUGH?

Many children quite naturally adapt their language depending on the situation they are in – even young children simplify their language when talking to toddlers, for example. It might therefore be thought that if teachers model Standard English, and children also hear and read it in many other contexts, all will be well and children will be able to switch without effort from one dialect to another. While this is the case for some, others find it very difficult to use forms other than the ones they have grown up with.

SHOULD WE CORRECT NON-STANDARD FORMS?

There are dangers in correcting children's spoken English. Partly, this is because it suggests we are more interested in grammar than in what children are trying to communicate. Also, children may think that we see the way they, their family and people in their community talk as inferior or wrong. That may then even lead to the opposite effect to the one intended: language is a badge of identity, and correction may make children even more resistant to changing the way they speak.

TEACHING KNOWLEDGE ABOUT LANGUAGE

If Standard English is taught as part of learning about language in all its richness and variety, then children are much more likely to be interested and to be willing to experiment with using different forms in different situations. Regional dialect forms, for example, may work very well in fiction, particularly in direct speech, to create a sense of place, time and character. Standard English in a debate or in a formal letter will convey the message more effectively because it is what people expect in such contexts. As children grow older and encounter a wider range of social situations, they are more likely to need to use Standard English. At school, they need to be able to use it to speak to the whole class and to adults, as well as in their writing. Other dialects are perfectly appropriate in less formal situations (e.g. at playtime or in small group activities).

Children who feel that their own language is recognised and valued are more likely to be happy to switch to Standard English when appropriate; it can be seen as a development from role play in the early years, when they enjoy trying out the language as well as the actions of different roles.

OVERGENERALISING OF RULES ABOUT STANDARD ENGLISH

Some speakers become so anxious about using Standard English that they overgeneralise what they see as rules and produce forms that may not be considered acceptable. Look at the following example to see how this can happen.

Grace and I had a cup of tea.	In Standard English, it is usual to place the other person first in a phrase that is the subject of the sentence. The pronoun is 'I' because it is the subject; it would be 'me' if it were the object (Sally hugged Grace and me).
Grace and me had a cup of tea.	Children often say this, or even 'me and Grace', placing themselves first.
Sally made tea for Grace and me.	Standard English uses 'me' here, as 'Grace and me' is the indirect object of the sentence.
Sally made tea for Grace and I.	This speaker has overcorrected; because 'Grace and me' is not Standard English as the subject of the sentence, she is unwilling to use it at all, even where Standard English does use it (as the object of the sentence). To check, try using the pronoun on its own. The speaker would be unlikely to say, 'Sally made tea for I' (although this form would be used in some regional dialects).
Sally made tea for Grace and myself.	This is another overcorrection; note that the speaker would be unlikely to say, 'Sally made tea for myself'.

STANDARD ENGLISH AND WRITING

Standard English is the variety used in almost all writing. For children, this can be a good way into noting and changing non-standard forms. Phrases such as 'In writing, we use …' or 'When we're writing, we put …' can be helpful here. Some children will, of course, absorb Standard English forms from their reading, along with many other features that characterise written as opposed to spoken English, and produce these spontaneously in their own writing, but others read relatively little, or seem able to encounter Standard English forms very frequently without adopting them in their own work.

CLASSROOM ACTIVITIES

INVESTIGATING DIALECT IN FICTION

RESOURCES

One or more fiction books at an appropriate level for the children, containing passages of dialogue using regional dialect (e.g. Frances Hodgson Burnett's *The Secret Garden*).

WHAT TO DO

Ask the children, working in pairs, to convert the dialect expressions to Standard English. Report back to the whole class: Have they changed words or grammar? What is the effect of the changes? It is important that the children can recognise non-standard forms and know what the equivalent standard form is, but also that they understand that the process may mean the text has lost colour and atmosphere, and that the characters are less interesting.

Note: This also works well with American authors such as Judy Blume – the whole narrative can be used rather than simply dialogue.

HERE IS THE NEWS

RESOURCES

Video extracts of news reports, transcripts of sections of the extracts, video cameras.

WHAT TO DO

Watch different newsreaders and reporters presenting the news. Discuss the language used: Who is the intended audience? Would the reporters talk in the same way before the broadcast began? Why do they have scripts?

Decide on some school news stories to report on. The children write their reports and present them to an editorial team, who will need to check for accuracy, interest and style, including the use of Standard English. The reports can then be recorded, viewed and evaluated.

REFERENCES

DfE (2012) *Teachers' Standards*. London: DFE.

DfE (2013) *The National Curriculum*. London: DfE.

FURTHER READING

Freeborn, D. (1993) *Varieties of English*. Basingstoke: Macmillan.

Hughes, A. (2012) *English Accents and Dialects*. London: Hodder.

Lockwood, M. (2005) 'Opening the wardrobe of voices: Standard English and language variation at Key Stage 2', in P. Goodwin (ed.), *The Literate Classroom*. London: Fulton.

Medwell, J. (2012) *Primary English Knowledge and Understanding*. London: SAGE.

Trudgill, P. (2000) *The Dialects of English*. Oxford: Blackwell.

3

DIALECT AND ACCENT

WHAT DO I NEED TO KNOW?

DIALECT

Languages have many varieties, often associated with different regions of a country. These different varieties, or dialects, can be identified by distinctive vocabulary and grammatical forms. Age and class, as well as geography, may affect the variety spoken; older speakers are more likely to use words and expressions unique to their locality, while more highly educated speakers are less likely to use regional dialect words and forms.

Different dialects also have a relatively small number of distinctive grammatical features. The following examples are taken from a number of different English dialects; some may sound odd to you, while others may be very familiar, depending on your own dialect:

I done the shopping before I come home.

The bus won't come while two o'clock.

I were looking for you everywhere.

I don't want no dinner.

That's the boy what done it.

He hurt hisself on the ice.

I put them books back on the bookshelf.

I had wrote my essay long before the deadline.

On the whole, these variations do not cause any difficulties in understanding. No dialect is more or less complex than any other, or more or less linguistically 'correct'. For example, it is sometimes argued that the fourth example above – a double negative – is 'wrong' because two negatives cancel each other out. If this were so, then presumably a triple negative ('I don't never want no dinner') would be acceptable. But English is not mathematics; multiple negatives are used in other languages, and they remain in some English dialects because they were used in Old English and Middle English.

ACCENT

Accent refers to the way that words are pronounced. For example, the vowel sound used in 'cup' is often the same as that used in 'foot' in the north of England, and many northern speakers do not use the vowel sound southern speakers use in 'cup' at all. In Liverpool, Manchester and Birmingham, the /g/ sound can be heard in words such as 'singer'.

Accents are typically associated with regions and cities, but speakers in each area do not sound exactly the same as each other; again, age and class may affect them. As an example, some young speakers in many areas use /f/ or /v/ in words such as 'with' and 'three', where older speakers do not.

As with dialects, there is an accent that does not have a geographical basis, sometimes described as 'BBC English'; this is received pronunciation (RP). Typically, a regional dialect will be spoken with the associated regional accent.

Received pronunciation is often considered to have more prestige than other accents, but even among regional accents some are considered to be more socially acceptable than others. We are more likely to hear newsreaders with Scottish accents than with Birmingham accents, for example.

To hear a range of regional dialects and accents from the UK, see **www.bl.uk/learning/langlit/ sounds/index.html**

WHAT IS IT USEFUL TO KNOW?

CHANGES IN DIALECTS OVER TIME

Dialect forms may change gradually over time. Sometimes regional dialects retain forms that used to be used all over the country. For example, all English dialects used to distinguish between you singular ('thou', 'thee') and you plural ('ye', 'you'). However, issues of politeness affected this usage; just as in French a stranger would not be addressed as *tu*, so 'you' came to be used for anyone not well known to the speaker, whether singular or plural, and the forms 'thee' and 'thou' disappeared from many dialects. They can still be found in northern areas: consider, for example, the well-known song 'On Ilkley Moor Baht 'at', which begins, neatly demonstrating both forms:

Wheear 'as tha bin sin ah saw thee?

In Liverpool, Irish immigrants brought with them their own way of showing whether one or more people were being addressed – 'you' is singular and 'youse' plural.

Dialect words also change over time, partly because so many are associated with traditional rural ways of life that have disappeared, and also because of the effect of increased mobility and mass media communication. In the past, for example, different words were used for 'girl' in different areas – 'maiden', 'mawther', 'wench'. Now only 'lass' remains, in the north.

CHANGES IN ACCENT OVER TIME

Accents are also subject to change over time. In the past, the /r/ sound was heard in words such as 'farm', 'car' and 'fork'; this gradually disappeared, starting in South East England, until today when it can only be found in pockets of Lancashire, East Anglia and the South West. Settlers in North America left England at a time when most speakers still had this accent feature, and Americans typically have kept it. Received pronunciation also changes over time, as radio and television broadcasts of the 1940s and 1950s demonstrate.

KEY KNOWLEDGE SUMMARY

Different dialects use different vocabulary and grammatical forms. They are usually associated with geographical areas. Accent refers to how words are pronounced, and again these are associated with different areas. Both dialects and accents change over time.

IN THE CLASSROOM

DIALECTS IN THE CLASSROOM

The most important influence on a child's language, after the early years, is the peer group. Children usually want to fit in, and that means sounding like their friends. Attempts in the past to get children who do not habitually use Standard English to do so have often been unsuccessful, whether the approach was encouragement or criticism. However, if children's own dialect is treated with respect and interest by teachers, it is more likely that they will be interested in learning to switch to Standard English in situations where it is appropriate.

For example, children may use dialect words that their teachers do not know, so they are then in the role of the expert, explaining how they use the word and whether there is a Standard English synonym. Listen to David Crystal explaining the history of the word 'mardy', which, unlike many dialect words, has spread geographically and is much more widely used now, thanks to its appearance in television soap operas: **www.bbc.co.uk/worldservice/learningenglish/radio/specials/1453_uptodate3/page13.shtml**

An interest in vocabulary is important both for reading comprehension, where the association between a wide vocabulary and good understanding is very strong, and for writing, where word choice is important in non-fiction, fiction and poetry writing.

ARE CHILDREN WHO SPEAK REGIONAL DIALECT DISADVANTAGED IN THE CLASSROOM?

It has to be recognised that children who speak Standard English at home are at an educational advantage in many ways. Children do need to be able to use Standard English when appropriate, and indeed it is a requirement in the National Curriculum (DfE, 2013).

ACCENTS IN THE CLASSROOM

It is important to note that no government guidance has ever suggested teachers should expect children to modify their regional accents. Regional accents are not lazy, careless or inferior; they are simply different from each other and from received pronunciation (RP). While it is true that some accents are less well regarded than others (particularly urban accents), they are a way in which speakers identify with their communities. Teachers should be careful not to make judgements about their pupils based on their accents.

It is sometimes argued that children will be disadvantaged in employment if they have regional accents. This is not necessarily so; call centres located in the North East were placed there precisely because speakers with the local accent are perceived as being friendly and trustworthy by callers from all over the country. In any case, trying to change children's accents is often unsuccessful, while if individuals decide for themselves later in life that they want to speak differently, they are usually able to modify their accents simply by trying to sound like models they have selected.

CLASSROOM ACTIVITIES

INVESTIGATING DIALECT WORDS

RESOURCES

None required.

WHAT TO DO

Ask the children to find out from friends and relations living in different parts of the country, or friends and neighbours who have moved into the area from other places, what words people in that place use for:

- bread rolls;
- truanting;
- a chasing game; and
- a picnic lunch.

Produce a chart or map to record the findings.

WHAT AM I LIKE?

RESOURCES

A clip from a film the children do not know, with a number of distinctive characters, such as *The Animals of Farthing Wood* or Nick Park's *Creature Comforts*.

WHAT TO DO

Play the clip, sound only, and ask children to listen to particular characters. What sort of character do they think this is, based on the speech? Now watch the clip. Does the character match their expectations? What additional clues are there when the character can be seen – expression, gesture, appearance?

Conclude with a discussion of whether we do judge people by how they sound (e.g. on the phone), and whether this is a good idea.

REFERENCE

DfE (2013) *The National Curriculum*. London: DfE.

FURTHER READING

Hughes, A. (2012) *English Accents and Dialects*. London: Hodder.

Trudgill, P. (1975) *Accent, Dialect and the School*. London: Edward Arnold.

Trudgill, P. (2000) *The Dialects of English*. Oxford: Blackwell.

4

FORMAL AND INFORMAL ENGLISH

WHAT DO I NEED TO KNOW?

FORMAL AND INFORMAL ENGLISH

It is easy to recognise the difference between formal and informal language, as the following examples from written and spoken English show:

> *The land has the benefit of the following rights reserved by a transfer of the land lying to the south and east of the land in this title.*

> *I had this weird dream ... it kind of creeped me out, you know?*

> *It gives me great pleasure to welcome our speaker, Alistair Stephenson, whose reputation in the field of environmentalism is known to you all.*

> *Just read Susie's message about M – is he OK? What happened? Where were you all?*

However, it would be wrong to think that all language, whether spoken or written, could be neatly categorised as formal or informal. In fact, there is a spectrum, from extremely formal to very informal, and language is matched to context. The term 'register' is used to mean language appropriate to a particular context, such as a doctor's appointment or a comedy show. Some social situations demand very formal language, which would be completely out of place in other contexts. The degree of formality is shown by a range of language features:

Vocabulary choice	In more formal situations, less common words are often used, such as 'prior to' instead of 'before'. There may also be specialised vocabulary such as, in a law court, 'plaintiff', 'prosecution' and 'verdict'. In informal situations, slang and swear words may be used, along with words such as 'thingy' or 'whatsit'.

(Continued)

(Continued)

Sentence structure	In more formal situations, sentences may be longer and more complex. In informal situations, sentences may be short, or if they are long, they are likely to be linked by simple conjunctions such as 'and' and 'so'. Speech in informal situations is characterised by many incomplete and minor sentences, such as: <ul><li>'I was going to - oh no.'</li><li>'Whatever.'</li><li>'If you must.'</li></ul> It is therefore often difficult to identify sentences in informal spoken language.
Text structure	More formal texts, whether spoken or written, are likely to be carefully structured, with a clear sequence, including an introduction and conclusion, and one point leading logically to another. Informal texts may jump from one topic to another, with the change of topic signalled briefly by a phrase such as 'By the way ...' or even 'Changing the subject ...'. Points may be returned to as new ideas arise.
Level of preparedness	Many written texts are produced relatively slowly, with much thought going into the composition. This is particularly the case for writing in formal contexts - reports, dissertations, published work. Less formal texts, including shopping lists, text messages and so on, are often written in haste and are unlikely to be reviewed. Of course, some spoken texts, such as speeches and presentations, may also be thoroughly prepared and scripted.
Fluency	Speech in informal situations is characterised by many false starts, such as 'Is it - do you ...'. It often also contains many 'fillers' such as 'I mean', 'like' and 'you know', which have no meaning but give the speaker thinking time. In more formal situations, such features would be inappropriate, and speech may be slower but will be more fluent.
Dialect choice	Standard English is the dialect used in formal situations, while many speakers use a regional dialect in informal situations.

WHAT IS IT USEFUL TO KNOW?

AUDIENCE AND PURPOSE

The degree of formality in language, whether in speech or in writing, depends on the audience and the purpose of the writing or talk. Language is usually less formal with a familiar audience such as family or friends. The purpose may be to inform, to persuade, to debate or to entertain. Even among the same group of people, language may switch from formal to informal depending on the purpose of the talk.

Consider, for example, a group of teachers in the staffroom after school. They spend ten minutes chatting about family matters and teasing each other. Then the staff meeting begins, with a discussion of pupil progress. The language shifts accordingly, from informal to a more formal register.

IS FORMAL LANGUAGE MORE COMPLEX?

It is sometimes thought that formal language is complex and difficult to understand, but it does not need to be. Indeed, if it is, it may not achieve its purpose. Taking time to prepare often means finding ways to express meanings as clearly, concisely and simply as possible. The Plain English Campaign fights for jargon-free and easy-to-understand language in official documents: **www.plainenglish.co.uk**

In contrast, informal language can be complex and difficult to follow as speakers are often formulating their ideas as they talk.

IS FORMAL LANGUAGE BORING?

Again, formal language does not need to be dull. In news reporting or speeches, for example, it is important that language is used effectively to engage the audience. This can involve:

- carefully considered vocabulary choices;

- use of imagery – metaphors and similes;

- use of well-chosen examples to illustrate general points; and

- language effects such as repetition and alliteration.

Language is chosen for impact, as can be seen in the following examples:

pitted against	*competing with*
brutally brief	*very short*
battling to bring about a truce	*working towards an agreement*

In contrast, informal language may be very boring if it is repetitive and includes much unnecessary detail, as in the following example:

> *So, I went to the doctor's on Tuesday – no, I tell a lie, it was Wednesday, Wednesday afternoon, that's right, and I didn't see the old doctor, it was the young one, the old one's gone part-time now …*

KEY KNOWLEDGE SUMMARY

Both spoken and written language vary along a spectrum from formal to informal, depending on the context. Standard English is used in formal contexts.

IN THE CLASSROOM

How realistic is it to expect primary-age children to use formal language with any degree of skill and confidence?

England's 2014 National Curriculum programme of study for English (DFE, 2013) states that children should choose the appropriate register in order to communicate effectively, and that in Years 3 to 4 they should be using language in a wider range of situations, for different audiences and purposes, including drama, formal presentations and debates.

SPEAKING

How successfully children will meet curriculum expectations is likely to depend on:

- experience of hearing formal language used in different situations and analysing it;

- regular opportunities to use formal language in a range of contexts; and

- focused feedback on their use of formal language.

WRITING

When faced with a writing task, children need to be clear about the audience and purpose, in order to judge how formal their writing should be. Children's attention should be drawn systematically, when reading and when writing, to features of formal language such as:

- conjuncts to link ideas such as 'although', 'nevertheless', 'in addition' and 'on the other hand';

- appropriate vocabulary choices ('when we arrived' rather than 'when we got there');

- use of punctuation such as colons and semicolons, while avoiding the use of exclamation marks; and

- avoidance of contractions such as 'isn't' and 'won't'.

VISITORS IN THE CLASSROOM

Visitors in school offer a valuable opportunity for children to practise a more formal conversational style. Preparation is often possible and can develop confidence. Lily, in a reception class, wrote the following questions for park rangers as an aide-memoire before a visit to a country park:

Is thay [there] toad sporn?

How do the toads have the toad sporn?

Way [why] do frogs liv in ponds?

How torl are the trees?

How high can frogs jump?

Wair is the pond?

It is unlikely that she would have been able to formulate this impressive range of questions without time to think and talk beforehand.

CLASSROOM ACTIVITIES

TEXT COLLECTIONS

RESOURCES

A text box is a collection of real texts – leaflets, flyers, postcards, poems, letters (both business and personal), lists, notices, epitaphs, posters, instructions, signs and so on. It provides models for children's own writing and resources for a range of activities.

WHAT TO DO

Ask the children, in pairs or groups, to select two texts to compare. Complete a comparison grid, looking at the intended audience, purpose and language features. What do the texts have in common? What are the differences, and why are they different?

ROLE PLAY

RESOURCES

Carefully chosen role-play areas provide rich opportunities for adults to model more formal language, which children can then use in their own play. Of course, some children may have significant real-life experience to draw on, but others do not, and books and role play with adults will need to provide a substitute.

WHAT TO DO

The language of many social situations such as shopping and hospital visits is semi-scripted in real life, with exchanges such as:

How can I help you?

I have an appointment.

Would you like to wait in the waiting room?

These can be modelled by adults, and children often enjoy adopting the language as well as the uniform and the behaviours of the different roles they try out.

REFERENCE

DfE (2013) *The National Curriculum*. London: DfE.

FURTHER READING

Alexander, R. (2004) *Towards Dialogic Teaching: Rethinking Classroom Talk*. Cambridge, MA: Dialogos.

Allott, K. and Waugh, D. (2016) *Language and Communication in Primary Schools*. London: SAGE.

DCSF (2003) *Speaking, Listening, Learning: Working with Children in Key Stages 1 and 2*. Nottingham: DCSF.

Eyre, I. (2007) *English for Primary and Early Years*. Milton Keynes: Open University Press.

Freeborn, D. (1993) *Varieties of English*. Basingstoke: Macmillan.

Neaum, S. (2012) *Language and Literacy for the Early Years*. London: SAGE.

5

PREFIXES

WHAT DO I NEED TO KNOW?

A *prefix* is a letter or group of letters placed before a root word.

For example, the word 'unlike' consists of the prefix 'un-' (meaning 'not') and the root (stem) word 'like'; the word 'unlike' means 'not like'.

In the word 'impossible', the prefix 'im-' is placed before possible to show that something is not possible.

Many prefixes in English are derived from Latin. Common ones include the following:

PREFIX	MEANING	EXAMPLES
de-	from, down, away, reverse, opposite	defuse, decommission
dis-	not, opposite, reverse, away	dislike, disprove
ex-	out of, away from	explosion, expel
il-	not	illegible, illegal
im-	not, without	immobile, improbable
in-	not, without	inoperable, inadvisable
mis-	bad, wrong	misunderstand, misspell
non-	not	non-fiction, nonentity
pre-	before	prenatal, prehistoric
pro-	for, forward, before	propose, pronoun
re-	again, back	revisit, revise
un-	against, not, opposite	unlike, unkind

For further examples, see **www.enchantedlearning.com/grammar/prefixsuffix/** and **www.bbc.co.uk/skillswise/factsheet/en17suff-e3-f-prefixes-and-suffixes**

WHAT IS IT USEFUL TO KNOW?

Numerical prefixes are useful additions to words to help us show how many of something there are. Many can be found in mathematics, and children will be familiar with triangles from early mathematics, and later quadrilaterals, pentagons, hexagons, heptagons, octagons and so on. The table below shows prefixes for different numbers together with examples. There are two different prefixes for some numbers because both the Latin and the Greek forms are used.

PREFIX MEANING	PREFIX	EXAMPLE WORDS
1	uni-	unicycle: cycle with one wheel
1	mono-	monologue: long speech by one person
2	bi-	bicycle: cycle with two wheels
3	tri-	tripod: three-legged stand
4	quad-	quadrangle: four-sided shape
5	quint-	quintuplets: five babies born at a single birth
5	penta-	pentathlon: athletic event with five activities
6	hex-	hexagon: six-sided shape
6	sex-	sextuplets: six babies born at a single birth
7	hept-	heptagon: seven-sided shape
7	sept-	septennial: lasting for or occurring every seven years
8	octo-	octogenarian: someone between 80 and 89 years old
9	novem-	November: formerly the ninth month of the year
10	deka- or deca-	decade: a period of ten years
hundred	cent-	century: a period of 100 years
hundred	hecto-	hectogram: 100 grams
thousand	milli-	millennium: a period of 1,000 years
thousand	kilo-	kilometre: 1,000 metres
million	mega-	megawatt: 1 million watts
billion	giga-	gigawatt: 1 billion watts

Notice how some of the prefixes that once referred to very specific numbers have come to be used in a more general way. Mega, for example, is used in megastar (a very big star) and we call a small invertebrate creature with lots of legs a millipede, even though most types have between 36 and 400 legs, and only one species has been discovered with 750!

For more examples, see **www.factmonster.com/ipka/A0774340.html**

KEY KNOWLEDGE SUMMARY

A prefix is a letter or group of letters placed before a root word. You should now understand that prefixes modify or qualify the meanings of words, so that, for example, 'unlike' means 'not like', a 'tricycle' is a 'cycle with three wheels', and 'prenatal' means 'before birth' and 'postnatal' means 'after birth'.

IN THE CLASSROOM

The English National Curriculum for England (DfE, 2013) requires children to understand the following about prefixes (and suffixes):

YEAR	
1	Add prefixes and suffixes: • using the spelling rule for adding -s or -es as the plural marker for nouns and the third-person singular marker for verbs • using the prefix un- • using -ing, -ed, -er and -est where no change is needed in the spelling of root words (e.g. helping, helped, helper, eating, quicker, quickest)
3-4	Apply their growing knowledge of root words, prefixes and suffixes (etymology and morphology) ... both to read aloud and to understand the meaning of new words they meet.
5-6	Apply their growing knowledge of root words, prefixes and suffixes (morphology and etymology) ... both to read aloud and to understand the meaning of new words that they meet.

Children meet prefixes in early talk, and may know and understand words such as dislike, unhappy and impossible long before they can read them.

An understanding of prefixes and suffixes is invaluable when children learn sets of words, as they do as part of the English National Curriculum. They can be taught how root words can be adapted to make other words. So, the first two words on the English National Curriculum list for Year 5–6 to learn are 'accommodate' and 'accompany'. Children can be shown how to use affixes to modify them and can then apply this knowledge and understanding when learning other vocabulary. For 'accommodate', they might also learn 'accommodation', 'accommodating', 'accommodated', 'accommodates' and 'unaccommodating'; for 'accompany', they might also learn 'accompanied', 'unaccompanied', 'accompanying' and so on.

Look at the following words for Year 3–4 and see how many more can be created by adding prefixes and/or suffixes: 'appear', 'answer', 'famous', 'grammar', 'mention'.

Some prefixes sound the same but have different meanings and can cause confusion for children. Two examples are provided below.

DIS- AND DYS-

Both 'dis-' and 'dys-' have similar meanings but they are not quite the same. 'Dis-' comes from Latin (apart). We use 'dis-' in the following ways:

- for negation – 'disadvantage';

- for reversal or absence – 'disappear';

- for removal or separation – 'disallow'; and

- to show completeness or intensification – 'disgruntled', 'disgusted'.

'Dis-' is also an example of a prefix that has come to be used as a word in its own right, with the word 'disrespect' having been shortened. 'Dys-' comes from Greek (bad, difficult or abnormal) and tends to appear in medical or scientific words. The word 'dyslexia' means difficulty with words. Other examples include 'dysfunctional', 'dyspeptic' and 'dyspraxia'.

'Dis-' is far more common than 'dys-'.

ANTI- AND ANTE-

Although these prefixes sound the same and are almost spelled the same, they have quite different meanings.

'Anti-' means against or opposite, and so we have words such as 'antibacterial' for something that acts against bacteria. 'Ante-' comes from Latin and means before, so 'antenatal' means before birth.

New words are often created using 'anti-' when people wish to show that they are opposed to things – anti-hunting, anti-war and recently anti-fracking.

CLASSROOM ACTIVITIES
WORD WINDOWS

You can adapt to focus on prefixes, suffixes or root words, or all three.

RESOURCES

You can do this on the computer by using PowerPoint with weblinks, but you can also use a few pieces of card and some pens to create word windows. Make some word cards for words that have prefixes, such as 'unhappy', 'dislike' and 'misplace'. Take one piece of A4-sized card and cut two lift-able flaps. Number the flaps 1 and 2. Staple the card to another piece of card so that word cards can be slid between the cards and revealed when the flaps are lifted.

WHAT TO DO

Divide the children into two teams and ask them to take turns to say which flap they would like to be lifted – flap 1 will reveal a word prefix and flap 2 a root word. They can then confer to guess what the whole word might be. For example, if 'place' were to be revealed when flap 2 was lifted, they might suggest 'misplace', 'replace' or even some words that don't exist. If they do this, ask them to suggest what the word might mean.

Develop the activity by having three flaps and words with three morphemes.

PREFIX AND ROOT WORD SNAP

This is a simple game to help children to focus on the meanings of prefixes and to reinforce their understanding of the ways in which bound and free morphemes come together to create words.

RESOURCES

Provide the children with sets of cards – some with prefixes on them and some with root words. Provide dictionaries for each group.

WHAT TO DO

Give the children time to check on the meanings of the prefixes by discussing them with neighbours and using dictionaries.

The children have a hand of cards each (say five, with the rest in a pile, face down, in the middle of the table) and place them on the table in front of them. One child places a card in the middle of the table and the person on his/her left has an opportunity to put another card with it to make a word. You can decide if you wish to allow compound words with no prefixes.

If the child can provide a card to create a word, he/she says 'snap', says the word and takes the 'trick', providing the other players agree that it is a real word. If there are any disputes, the children should refer to the dictionaries.

If a child cannot find a card to create a word, the next player on the left has a try, and so on. If no one can make a word, the player who put the card down first should take a card from the middle of the table and see if that will make a word. If not, the next player takes one, and so on. When no more words can be made, the tricks are counted. All the created words should be written down and a list provided so that you can check for misconceptions and share interesting words with the class.

For interactive activities, see **www.bigbrownbear.co.uk/demo/prefix.htm**

REFERENCE

DfE (2013) *The National Curriculum*. London: DfE.

FURTHER READING

Waugh, D., Warner, C. and Waugh, R. (2019) *Teaching Grammar, Punctuation and Spelling in Primary Schools* (3rd edition). London: SAGE, Chapter 2.

6

SUFFIXES

WHAT DO I NEED TO KNOW?

Just as we can create new words and modify the meanings of words by putting prefixes at the beginning (see Chapter 5), we can also add groups of letters to the end of words to make new words. For example, if we take the word 'work', we can add:

- '-s' to make 'works';

- '-er' to make 'worker';

- '-ing' to make 'working'; and

- '-ed' to make 'worked'.

There are two ways in which suffixes can make new words:

1. When we use a suffix to change a word grammatically, for example from singular to plural ('dog' to 'dogs', 'watch' to 'watches') or from present to past tense ('watch' to 'watched', 'skip' to 'skipped'), we are using an *inflectional suffix*.

2. When we use a suffix to create new meaning ('work' to 'worker', 'beauty' to 'beautiful'), we are using a *derivational suffix*.

INFLECTIONAL SUFFIXES

Although suffixes are used to ensure phrases and sentences are grammatically correct, inflectional suffixes don't change the meaning of the original words.

SUFFIX	ORIGINAL WORD	WORD WITH SUFFIX ADDED	GRAMMATICAL CHANGE MADE
-s	book	books	plural
-es	match	matches	plural
-en/-ren	ox	oxen	irregular plural
	child	children	

-s	I like	she likes	third-person singular
-es	I watch	he watches	third-person singular
-ed	I look	looked	past tense
			past participle
-en	I take	he has taken	past participle (irregular)
-ing	I go	she is going	continuous/progressive
-er	tall	taller	comparative
-est	tall	the tallest	superlative

DERIVATIONAL SUFFIXES

Derivational suffixes change the meanings of words even though the new meaning is related to or derived from the old meaning. When we use suffixes in this way, we often change the word class (or part of speech) of words when we add suffixes. For example, in the sentence 'Jill was a careful driver', 'careful' is an adjective to describe the driver. But if we add '-ly' to 'careful', we get 'carefully'. We couldn't say 'Jill was a carefully driver', but we could say 'Jill drives carefully'. By adding the suffix '-ly', we change an adjective into an adverb.

Look at the sentences below and decide which word class each of the underlined words belongs to:

Demi was an <u>honest</u> girl.

Demi was well known for her <u>honesty</u>.

Frances made a <u>fool</u> of herself.

Frances behaved <u>foolishly</u>.

In the first sentence, 'honest' describes 'girl' and is an adjective. In the second, by adding '-y', 'honest' becomes a noun (an abstract noun).

In the third sentence, 'fool' is a noun, but when we add '-ish' and '-ly' we create an adverb to show how Frances behaved. Notice how we can add more than one suffix to some words. For example:

origin – original – originally

person – personal – personalise/personality

hope – hopeful – hopefulness/hopefully

When a suffix that starts with a vowel is added to a word that ends with a silent '-e', the '-e' usually disappears in the spelling of the new word. For example, we say:

noteworthy,   *but notable*

statement,   *but stating*

lately,   *but latest*

There are a few exceptions in words where losing the '-e' would change the pronunciation (e.g. 'noticeable' and 'ageing').

Try the rule out by adding suffixes to base words – this could be done as a game with words and suffixes on sets of cards, to create both real and new words.

WHAT IS IT USEFUL TO KNOW?

There are several hundred derivational suffixes. Here are some of the more common ones:

SUFFIX	EXAMPLE OF ORIGINAL WORD	EXAMPLE WITH SUFFIX ADDED	CHANGE IN WORD CLASS
-ation	inform	information	verb to noun
-sion	revise	revision	verb to noun
-er	teach	teacher	verb to noun
-cian	optic	optician	remains a noun
-ess	prince	princess	remains a noun
-ness	good	goodness	adjective to noun
-al	remove	removal	verb to noun
-ary	mission	missionary	remains a noun
-ment	state	statement	verb to noun
-y	dirt	dirty	noun to adjective
-al	department	departmental	noun to adjective
-able	drink	drinkable	noun to adjective
-ly	friend	friendly	noun to adjective
-y	fish	fishy	noun to adjective
-ful	hope	hopeful	noun to adjective
-ly	helpful	helpfully	adjective to adverb

For a much longer and more comprehensive list, see **www.learnthat.org/pages/view/suffix.html**

For each of the examples provided, try to think of other words that use the same suffix. For example, for '-ful', you might choose 'doubtful', 'useful', 'remorseful' and so on; for '-al', you might choose 'formal', 'normal', 'digital' and so on.

This kind of activity can work well with children and helps them to see spelling generalisations.

COMMON SUFFIXES

There are many common suffixes in English; a fairly comprehensive list can be found at **http://grammar.about.com/od/words/a/comsuffixes.htm**

Work with children to assemble a list; look at words with a common suffix to decide what each one means and how it changes the meaning of the base word. For example, thinking about the words 'punishment', 'contentment' and 'refreshment' might lead to the conclusion that '-ment' implies 'the result' of the base word, while 'foolish', 'fortyish' and 'laddish' show that '-ish' means 'rather like' the base word.

KEY KNOWLEDGE SUMMARY

A suffix is a group of letters added to the end of a word. It may modify the meaning of the root word by making a noun plural, for example, or changing a verb into the past tense. Other suffixes may change the class of a word (e.g. making a noun into a verb or an adjective into an adverb). Most suffixes have regular patterns.

IN THE CLASSROOM

The English National Curriculum requires children to understand suffixes from Year 1 onwards (DfE, 2013). Whichever curriculum you teach, it will be useful to note the progression in the English curriculum:

Y1	Regular *plural noun suffixes* -s or -es (e.g. *dog, dogs*; *wish, wishes*), including the effects of these suffixes on the meaning of the noun.
	Suffixes that can be added to *verbs* where no change is needed in the spelling of root words (e.g. *helping, helped, helper*).
Y2	Formation of *nouns* using *suffixes* such as *-ness, -er* and by compounding (e.g. *whiteboard, superman*).
	Formation of *adjectives* using *suffixes* such as *-ful, -less*.
	Use of the *suffixes -er, -est* in *adjectives* and *-ly* to turn adjectives into *adverbs*.
Y5	Converting *nouns* or *adjectives* into *verbs* using *suffixes* (e.g. *-ate; -ise; -ify*).

The English National Curriculum includes prescribed lists of words that children must learn and be able to spell (DfE, 2013). Whichever words you teach children to spell, it is important that they understand how they can make other words from most words by adding prefixes and/or suffixes. By discussing these with children, you enable them to learn several more words for most of those they learn, as well as showing them how words are built so that they can apply this knowledge and understanding when they meet new words.

Children often have difficulty with spelling the many varieties of the suffix pronounced 'shun'. There are some rules that can help:

- '-cian' – where words end in 'c'; common occupations;

- '-tion' – the most common ending;

- '-sion' – where the base word ends in 'd'/'de' or 's'/'se' (e.g. 'explode', 'confuse');

- '-ssion' – clear soft 'sh' sound;

- '-ation' – long 'a' is always followed by '-tion';

- '-otion'/'-ution'/'-etion' – the base word usually contains the vowel, clearly pronounced; and

- '-ution' – words are usually longer than three syllables, '-usion' tends to be shorter.

For an exercise, see **www.saintambrosebarlow.wigan.sch.uk/Y5Spelling/suffixes2Y5t2. htm**

EXTENSION ACTIVITY

See how many words you can find where spellings follow the rules described above. Use a dictionary to help you. Write down a sentence for each of the words to show that you understand the rule.

Children can enjoy practising the use of suffixes by making sentences including as many different versions as possible of one 'root' word:

I love my love because she is lovely, and she has a lovable face and a loving family.

His faithful dog doggedly dogged his footsteps, giving little doggy snuffles.

CLASSROOM ACTIVITIES

SPELLING INVESTIGATIONS

An activity that helps children to learn spellings and to learn about spelling and vocabulary.

RESOURCES

Choose some appropriate words for children to learn. In England, these might be drawn from the prescribed lists in the National Curriculum. Provide lists for each group, varying the words provided according to children's abilities.

WHAT TO DO

Talk with the whole class about the ways in which suffixes can be added to words to modify their meaning. Provide some examples and leave these on display.

Ask the children to look carefully at the words they have been given and to use look/say/cover/ write/check to learn them. Encourage them to identify the 'tricky' parts of words and to focus on them.

Challenge each group to find as many words as possible that can be created by adding suffixes to their words. Encourage them to check these in a dictionary to ensure they exist. Where the children create words that do not exist, talk with them about what the words might mean, and explain that new words are created all the time and so one day their word even might appear in the dictionary.

Bring the class together to share what they have found. Write some of the words on the board and discuss their spellings and meanings. Discuss generalisations that can be made about spelling when adding suffixes, including such things as what happens when '-ed' or '-ing' are added.

Follow the lesson up by asking the children to collect suffixes in their reading and list some of the words they found. They could also look at adverts, signs and notices to find examples. Make a display of words with suffixes and include photographs.

REFERENCE

DfE (2013) *The National Curriculum*. London: DfE.

FURTHER READING

Waugh, D., Warner, C. and Waugh, R. (2019) *Teaching Grammar, Punctuation and Spelling in Primary Schools* (3rd edition). London: SAGE, Chapter 2.

USEFUL WEBSITE

For information on suffixes, see **www.englishclub.com/vocabulary/suffixes.htm**

7

COMPOUND WORDS

WHAT DO I NEED TO KNOW?

WHAT IS A COMPOUND WORD?

A compound word is formed from two or more other words (e.g. 'bedroom' from 'bed' and 'room', 'head teacher', from 'head' and 'teacher').

Compound words may be written in three different ways:

1. As one word: 'bathroom', 'lunchbox', 'toothbrush'.

2. Hyphenated: 'cover-up', 'break-up', 'play-off', 'risk-taker'.

3. As two words – 'pocket money', 'question mark', 'pop music'.

Most compound words are nouns, but some are adjectives or verbs:

*   Nouns include 'coffee table', 'haircut' and 'screwdriver'.

*   Adjectives include 'breathtaking', 'homesick' and 'awe-inspiring'.

*   Verbs include 'rubber-stamp', 'overtake' and 'sunbathe'.

The words that make up a compound word must each be able to stand alone, so 'hairdo' is made up of 'hair' and 'do'. This distinguishes compound words from those that are created by adding prefixes or suffixes to existing words. For example, 'hairy' is made up of 'hair', which can stand alone, and the suffix '-y', which cannot, and 'doing' is made up of 'do', which can stand alone, and the suffix '-ing', which cannot.

When we separate words into units of meaning in this way, we are separating them into morphemes, which are individual units of meaning. Morphemes that can stand alone are called free morphemes, and those that cannot are called bound morphemes, because they need to be bound to another morpheme to have meaning. Look at the words below and separate them into morphemes, and decide which morphemes are free and which are bound:

sunflower

flowery

doormat

doors

'Sunflower' ('sun' + 'flower') and 'doormat' ('door' + 'mat') are made up of two free morphemes, while 'flowery' ('flower' + 'y') and 'doors' ('door' + 's') each have a free morpheme ('flower' and 'door') and a bound morpheme ('-y' and '-s'). So, 'sunflower' and 'doormat' are compound words, but 'flowery' and 'doors' are not.

WHAT IS THE DIFFERENCE BETWEEN COMPOUND WORDS AND DERIVATIVES?

Compound words are made up of other words. Words such as 'triangle', 'usually' and 'replace' are made up of a word plus a bound morpheme, such as a prefix or a suffix, and are called derivatives. So, 'triangle' is 'tri' + 'angle', but 'tri-' cannot stand alone as a word. The same is true for '-ly' at the end of 'usual' and 're-' at the beginning of 'replace'.

WHAT IS IT USEFUL TO KNOW?

Compound words can be written in three different formats.

OPEN FORM

Words are not joined and do not have hyphens, but fit together as single entities: 'bus stop', 'prime minister', 'Swiss roll', 'rock star'.

CLOSED FORM

Words are joined together as one word: 'football', 'hairbrush', 'handbag'. Some words that now use the closed form once used a hyphenated form.

HYPHENATED FORM

Examples include: 'my son-in-law', 'a two-year-old', 'the best-known'.

When compounded with other modifiers, adjectives (see Chapters 12 and 13) are often hyphenated: 'the best-paid job', 'short-term gains', 'half-baked ideas'.

Some people are confused about when to use hyphens for people's ages. In 'a ten-year-old girl', hyphens should be used, but when the age comes after the person and we *don't* use an article (a, an or the), hyphens are not needed:

The girl is ten years old, but she is a ten-year-old.

I have a five-year-old son. My son is five years old.

SUSPENDED COMPOUNDS

We also sometimes see suspended compounds, as in 'the full- and part-time staff' and 'the first-, second- and third-placed runners won prizes'.

KEY KNOWLEDGE SUMMARY

WHAT IS A COMPOUND WORD?

A compound word is made up of two or more other words, each of which is a free morpheme – a unit that can stand on its own. Words made with prefixes and suffixes are not compound words.

Compound words may be written as one word, hyphenated, or as two separate words.

IN THE CLASSROOM

The English National Curriculum for England (DfE, 2013) only mentions compound words for Year 2: formation of nouns using suffixes such as '-ness' and '-er' and by compounding (e.g. 'whiteboard', 'superman'). However, the document's glossary does state:

Compounding is very important in English.

(p87)

For many children, an introduction to compound words may provide their first experience and understanding of the component parts of words. This understanding is vital both for developing an ability to decode meaning from words and for spelling. By breaking words into meaningful parts, we are able to apply our existing knowledge to unfamiliar vocabulary.

New compound words are constantly being created, sometimes for new inventions or activities. The 2013 edition of the *Oxford Dictionary Online* included the following for the first time:

vom-worthy

double denim

chandelier earring

flat forms

food baby

babymoon

digital detox

To find out more, see **https://public.oed.com/updates/**

For a series of lists of compound words, see **www.learningdifferences.com/Main%20 Page/Topics/Compound%20Word%20Lists/Compound_Word_%20Lists_complete. htm**

Sometimes children and people learning English can be confused when words that can go together in a phrase are used in a compound, and vice versa. For example, in the sentence 'I saw a black bird', the bird could be any kind of bird that is black. But if we change the sentence to 'I saw a blackbird', the bird is now a particular species – a blackbird. In a phrase, we tend to stress the second word (in this case, 'bird'), but in a compound word we tend to stress the first part. Try saying the two versions of the sentence to see how this works. Now try saying each of the following and decide where the main stress is in the underlined words:

I wrote on the <u>whiteboard</u>.

I wrote on the <u>white board</u>.

She wore a <u>lightweight</u> jacket.

She could easily lift the <u>light weight</u>.

This can lead to jokes:

How do you make a Swiss roll?

Push him down a hill.

What kind of nails do carpenters avoid?

Fingernails.

What part of a newspaper do angry people like best?

The crossword puzzle.

CLASSROOM ACTIVITIES

COMPOUND WORD SNAP

A matching game that can be played as a class or in groups to develop an understanding of compound words.

RESOURCES

Make a set of word cards that could be combined with other words to create compound words. The following may be useful:

foot	bag	hand	ball	ache	teacher
play	house	ground	case	book	road
head	cross	suit	sauce	pan	bin
brush	dust	hair	mower	man	lawn
post	wash	eye	top	lap	box

WHAT TO DO

Give each child a card and ensure that everyone can read the words. Ask one child to hold up a word and ask if anyone has a word that could go with it to make a new, compound word. Continue and award a point to the class for every compound word created within a set time. Write the words on the board so that you can look through them with the children afterwards.

Have a good dictionary available and/or a computer spellchecker so that words can be checked to see if they exist. Where the children suggest a word that does not appear in the dictionary, invite the class to suggest what the word might mean. For example, a 'lawnteacher' might show you how to grow grass, while a 'hairmower' could be used to cut a giant's hair! You might also explain that even though the words do not exist in dictionaries at the moment, they might in the future, as new words are being created all the time.

Encourage the children to look for compound words in their reading, and play the game again, challenging the class to beat the previous number of words created in the same amount of time.

MAKE COLLECTIONS OF COMPOUND WORDS

Encourage children to look for compound words in their reading and to explore different topics to find examples.

RESOURCES

Books, web access, a good dictionary.

WHAT TO DO

Show some examples of compound words from different categories, activities and subject areas. These might include some of the following:

GENERAL NATURE	TRANSPORT	JOBS	SPORT	BIRDS
waterfall	bus stop	police officer	football	blackbird
moonlight	skateboard	fireman	wicketkeeper	greenfinch
sunbeam	lorryload	dressmaker	quarterback	wagtail
daylight	signal box	lifeguard	batsman	woodpecker
butterfly	hubcap	care-worker	goalkeeper	kingfisher
sunflower	gearstick	newsreader	scrumhalf	yellowhammer

Talk with the children about how the compounds are sometimes formed by putting two words together and sometimes by hyphenating them. Give different groups of children different topics and ask them to explore books, including indexes, to find as many compound terms as they can within a given time.

Afterwards, challenge them to add to their collections at home or in any free time when they are at school.

For compound word games, see **www.learninggamesforkids.com/vocabulary_games/ compound-words.html** and **www.vocabulary.co.il/pdf_files/lesson_plans/compound wordlessonplan.pdf**

REFERENCE

DfE (2013) *The National Curriculum*. London: DfE.

FURTHER READING

Waugh, D., Warner, C. and Waugh, R. (2019) *Teaching Grammar, Punctuation and Spelling in Primary Schools* (3rd edition). London: SAGE.

USEFUL WEBSITES

For help deciding whether a compound should be written as one word, separate words or hyphenated words, see **www.merriam-webster.com/help/faq/compound.htm**

For more information on compound words, see **http://grammar.ccc.commnet.edu/grammar/ compounds.htm**

For a fascinating examination of compound words that Charles Dickens may (or may not) have invented, see **www.worldwidewords.org/articles/ar-dic1.htm**

8

PLURALS

WHAT DO I NEED TO KNOW?

Most nouns can be singular, to indicate there is one of something, or plural, when there is more than one (e.g. 'book' and 'books', 'cow' and 'cows'). Nouns usually become plurals by adding '-s' to the end (e.g. 'dog'/'dogs', 'monkey'/'monkeys'). Some add '-es' to make a plural (e.g. 'match'/'matches', 'box'/'boxes'). We can make generalisations about the way in which many plurals are made, and this can be helpful when teaching and learning spelling.

NOUNS ENDING IN '-CH', '-S', '-SH', '-X' OR '-Z'

If the noun ends with '-ch', '-s', '-ss', '-sh', '-x' or '-z', add '-es' to form the plural:

SINGULAR	PLURAL
match	matches
kiss	kisses
fox	foxes

An exception to this generalisation occurs when the '-ch' ending is pronounced with a /k/ sound – you add '-s' rather than '-es':

SINGULAR	PLURAL
stomach	stomachs
loch	lochs

There are very few commonly used words with this sound for '-ch', but you can find examples at **http://rattanji.blogspot.co.uk/2011/07/english-words-ending-in-ch-140-ch-makes. html#!/2011/07/english-words-ending-in-ch-140-ch-makes.html**

NOUNS ENDING IN '-Y'

Nouns that end with a consonant plus '-y' become plural by changing '-y' to '-ies':

SINGULAR	PLURAL
lady	ladies
pony	ponies
dictionary	dictionaries

Nouns that end with a vowel before '-y' simply add an '-s':

SINGULAR	PLURAL
monkey	monkeys
day	days
boy	boys

NOUNS ENDING IN '-F' OR '-FE'

Nouns ending in a consonant or a single vowel plus '-f' or '-fe' usually change the '-f' or '-fe' to '-ves':

SINGULAR	PLURAL
knife	knives
half	halves
thief	thieves
wife	wives
leaf	leaves

There are exceptions to this generalisation, including 'chief'/'chiefs', but note that here the sound in the plural is still /f/ rather than /v/.

NOUNS ENDING IN '-O'

Nouns ending in '-o' present a problem in English because there is no reliable rule or logic to their plurals. Some just add an '-s', some add '-es', and there are many words where either form is acceptable.

Where the final '-o' has another vowel immediately before it, the extra 'e' is not used (e.g. 'zoo' and 'studio' become 'zoos' and 'studios'). In other cases, words have to be learned individually. Some nouns ending in '-o' add '-es' in the plural:

SINGULAR	PLURAL
buffalo	buffaloes
domino	dominoes
echo	echoes
embargo	embargoes
hero	heroes
mosquito	mosquitoes
potato	potatoes
tomato	tomatoes
torpedo	torpedoes
veto	vetoes

And just to complicate things, some nouns ending in '-o' can be spelled with either '-s' or '-es' when plural:

SINGULAR	PLURAL
banjo	banjos *or* banjoes
cargo	cargos *or* cargoes
flamingo	flamingos *or* flamingoes
fresco	frescos *or* frescoes
ghetto	ghettos *or* ghettoes
halo	halos *or* haloes
mango	mangos *or* mangoes
memento	mementos *or* mementoes
motto	mottos *or* mottoes
tornado	tornados *or* tornadoes
volcano	volcanos *or* volcanoes

WHAT IS IT USEFUL TO KNOW?

NO CHANGE FOR THE PLURAL

Some words remain the same in the plural as the singular. These include many types of animals (e.g. 'sheep', 'deer', 'bison'), 'fish' and individual species of fish (e.g. 'trout', 'cod', 'salmon', 'herring'), and words such as 'aircraft', 'offspring', 'species' and 'you'.

There are also words that do not have a plural because they refer to a group of things, and are not 'count nouns' of which it makes sense to talk in the plural. Examples of these are 'weather', 'wheat' and 'corn'.

Seven nouns change their vowel in the plural: 'foot'/'feet', 'tooth'/'teeth', 'man'/'men', 'woman'/'women', 'goose'/'geese', 'mouse'/'mice' and 'louse'/'lice'.

IMPORTED NOUNS AND THEIR PLURALS

Nouns from foreign languages often cause problems, with some retaining the plural form from their original language ('radius'/'radii', 'crisis'/'crises') and others changing to a more anglicised version ('chorus'/'choruses'), while others seem to have two acceptable plurals ('cactuses' and 'cacti').

Both Latin and Greek neuter nouns have plural forms in '-a'.

We have become used to 'criterion'/'criteria' and 'phenomenon'/'phenomena', but it is not always recognised that 'data' is the plural of 'datum' (something that is given) and 'media' is the plural of 'medium' (something through which information is passed). It is common to see such sentences as 'The data is unreliable' or 'The media has been blamed', which are technically incorrect, even though they are commonly used.

Words from other modern languages are usually just adopted into English morphology (e.g. 'brat-wursts', 'vodkas', 'cappuccinos'). An exception is made for the French '-eau' ending – we talk of 'gateaux' and 'tableaux'.

KEY KNOWLEDGE SUMMARY

Plurals can be formed in many different ways, as you can see above. How does each of the following words form its plural? What rules or generalisations, if any, can you use to help remember these?

- donkey
- church
- mackerel
- potato
- knife
- chair
- criterion

IN THE CLASSROOM

Perhaps surprisingly, given some of the complexities and irregularities associated with plurals, the English National Curriculum for England (DfE, 2013) does not give much attention to irregular plurals except where these require apostrophes to show possession:

YEAR	REQUIRED KNOWLEDGE AND UNDERSTANDING
1	Regular *plural noun suffixes* -s or -es (e.g. *dog, dogs; wish, wishes*), including the effects of these suffixes on the meaning of the noun.
4	The grammatical difference between *plural* and *possessive* -s.

Children can be confused about the spelling of even simple plurals, because we tend to pronounce the '-s' and '-es' ending differently for different words.

The final '-s' in many words (e.g. 'dogs', 'matches', 'witches', 'trees') has a /z/ sound as in 'zero'. Sometimes this leads to spellings such as 'dogz', 'matchuz', 'witchuz' and 'treez'.

Irregular plurals can lead to misconceptions for children and people learning English as a second language, who sometimes apply the rule they know best by adding '-s' or '-es' to all nouns in the plural. This leads to errors such as 'mans', 'sheeps', 'mouses' and 'tooths' for irregular plurals.

Try making collections of plurals and displaying them in your classroom. Ask the children to add to lists as they discover new ones in their reading, and add others yourself whenever the children make mistakes.

When a singular noun is made plural in a sentence, it can have an effect on other words such as verbs, determiners and pronouns. Shared work on changing singulars to plurals in sentences will not only develop children's understanding of pluralisation; it will also help them consider grammar and syntax. For example, look at the sentences below and in each case change the underlined noun to its plural form. What else do you need to do to the sentences so that they make sense and are grammatically accurate?

A *train* was late.

John's *dog* is his best friend and it goes everywhere with him.

In the first sentence, we need to change 'a' to 'the' or 'some', or omit the determiner altogether, and change 'was' to 'were':

The/some trains were late. Or *Trains were late.*

In the second sentence, when 'dog' becomes 'dogs', we need to change 'is' to 'are', 'friend' to 'friends', 'goes' to 'go' and 'it' to 'they':

John's *dogs are his best friends and they go everywhere with him.*

Some words only exist in the plural form, including 'scissors', 'trousers', 'binoculars' and 'jeans'. These tend to be items that have two parts, and we often use 'a pair of' with them.

There are also other words that end with '-s' but are only ever used as plurals, such as 'amends', 'outskirts', 'congratulations', 'stairs', 'news' and 'remains'.

Finally, there are words with a 'zero ending' (no '-s' or other affix) that are always plural, including 'cattle', 'police', 'poultry', 'livestock' and 'people'.

Collective nouns are used to refer to a group of something, and include 'flock' for sheep and so on, 'herd' for cows and so on, and some delightful – though not so common – ones such as 'a kindle of kittens', 'a colony of penguins' and 'a murder of crows'.

CLASSROOM ACTIVITIES

COLLECTING PLURALS

This activity can be focused or incidental – that is, children could be asked to look in texts for examples of plurals as a specific activity, or they could be asked to look out for them during their reading over a period of time.

RESOURCES

Lots of texts.

WHAT TO DO

Ask the children to find examples of plurals and to note these on a list. This might be a group list or a list for a pair of children, but this activity is best done collaboratively so that the children have opportunities to discuss their findings.

Once a list has been compiled, ask the children to classify their plurals. You could use different headings according to their levels of understanding, but the following might be useful:

- Words in which the plural is formed by adding '-s'.

- Words in which the plural is formed by adding '-es'.

- Words in which the singular and plural are the same (e.g. 'cod', 'sheep').

- Irregular plurals such as 'men', 'mice' and 'feet'.

- Words that are always plural (e.g. 'trousers', 'binoculars').

- Collective nouns (e.g. 'herd', 'flock', 'set', 'bundle').

Draw the class together and ask the children to share their examples. This will give you an opportunity to discuss different plural forms and to talk about spelling generalisations. You will also be able to note any misconceptions and plan to address these in future lessons.

REFERENCE

DfE (2013) *The National Curriculum*. London: DfE.

FURTHER READING

Crystal, D. (2004) *Rediscover Grammar* (3rd edition). Harlow: Longman.

Waugh, D., Warner, C. and Waugh, R. (2019) *Teaching Grammar, Punctuation and Spelling in Primary Schools* (3rd edition). London: SAGE.

9

WORD CLASSES

WHAT DO I NEED TO KNOW?

Look at the sentence below:

Rovers beat Brentford.

Each word in the sentence has a role. 'Rovers' and 'Brentford' are special names (proper nouns) and tell us who was involved; 'beat' is a verb that tells us what happened. Now look at the sentence below:

Fantastic Rovers beat gallant Brentford.

Now we have the words 'fantastic' and 'gallant' to describe the two teams. These are adjectives. We can add to the sentence:

Fantastic Rovers narrowly beat gallant Brentford.

'Narrowly' tells us how Rovers beat Brentford and is an adverb. We could go on. The important thing to remember is:

Every <u>word</u> belongs to a word class which summarises the ways in which it can be used in grammar. The major word classes for English are: <u>noun</u>, <u>verb</u>, <u>adjective</u>, <u>adverb</u>, <u>preposition</u>, <u>determiner</u>, <u>pronoun</u>, <u>conjunction</u>. Word classes are sometimes called 'parts of speech'.

(DfE, 2013, p84)

You will find out more about the word classes above in separate chapters, but why is it important that we can identify and name them? Consider the reasons suggested below:

- For teachers in most countries, the curriculum requires children to know and understand the terms.

- When we discuss texts, we can focus on different aspects, using a common terminology to appreciate the qualities of the writing.

- When we learn another language, we need to know and understand word classes. You may remember learning to conjugate verbs in French, Spanish or German.

- We use correct terminology in other subjects such as mathematics. Did you ever tell children to 'draw a three-sided shape with three lines that join at corners and with every corner and line the same size'? No? But you may well have asked them to draw an equilateral triangle.

Look at the 'sentence' below and decide what is wrong with it:

Rovers in the last minute.

Without a verb between the proper noun 'Rovers' and the preposition 'in', we don't know what Rovers did in the last minute. You could remove other words from the sentence and ask children to suggest appropriate words to complete it, all the time ensuring that you use the correct terminology.

The first section may have seemed very simple to you, and usually that is the case once we understand word classes. However, there is a complication: words do not always belong to the same classes. Look at the two sentences below and decide which word class 'house' belongs to in each:

I live in a small house in Durham.

We need to house homeless people.

In the first sentence, 'house' is a common noun – the name of something. In the second sentence, 'house' is a verb – something to be done.

WHAT IS IT USEFUL TO KNOW?

WORD CLASS MOBILITY

There are three criteria for deciding which class a word belongs to:

1. The meaning of a word.

2. The form of a word.

3. The position of a word in a sentence.

1. THE MEANING OF A WORD

This is the traditional way of classifying words by defining them, using terms such as 'doing word' or 'describing word'.

However, it is not infallible. Look at these sentences:

Time flies like an arrow.

Fruit flies like a banana.

In the first sentence, 'flies' is the verb and 'like' is an adverb. In the second sentence, 'Fruit flies' are the subject, a noun phrase, and 'like' is the verb.

2. THE FORM OR 'SHAPE' OF A WORD

Many words in English have a form, or *morphology*, that shows what class they belong to. For instance, words ending in '-ness' are nouns: 'greatness', 'sadness', 'cheerfulness', 'loneliness'.

Other common noun-endings are '-tion' and '-ity': 'action', 'distraction', 'station', 'completion', 'simplicity', 'calamity', 'felicity', 'humidity'.

Many adverbs end in '-ly': 'happily', 'correctly', 'wrongly', 'badly'.

And many adjectives end in '-like' or '-able'/'-ible': 'cow-like', 'doglike', 'tent-like', 'miserable', 'accessible', 'believable'.

However, such clues are not always reliable. 'Lovely' is not an adverb, but an adjective. Many '-tion' nouns are frequently used as verbs (e.g. 'I need to condition my hair').

The inflected endings of '-s' to mark plural nouns, as well as '-ed' or '-ing' to show parts of verbs, are also clues that can give guidance when classifying word classes by the form of a word.

3. THE POSITION OR 'ENVIRONMENT' OF A WORD IN A SENTENCE

This way of categorising the word classes by looking at the word in the specific context of a sentence is probably the most useful and reliable.

For instance, compare:

I walk to school every day.

On Sundays we often have a walk.

It is easy to see that the word 'walk' is a verb in the first sentence (it is preceded by a subject and followed by two adverbial phrases). If we were to substitute this word with another, we would have to choose another verb. In the second example, however, we would need another noun or noun phrase.

The English language has many words that can belong to more than one class (e.g. 'light', 'burn', 'hide', 'play', 'break'). In addition, there is an increasing tendency to coin new usages which use a verb as a noun, such as:

It's a big ask. *(instead of 'demand')*

Can you give me a quote? *(instead of 'quotation')*

These words that are used in more than one class are sometimes called *open-class items*. Words that can be used in only one class are known as *closed-class items*.

KEY KNOWLEDGE SUMMARY

WHAT ARE WORD CLASSES?

This is the term for the roles that words play in a sentence – terms such as 'noun', 'verb', 'adjective' and 'adverb', which are sometimes called 'parts of speech'. Many words, especially nouns and verbs, can be used in more than one different class, and increasingly there is movement in usage observed in the media. This is called 'word class mobility'.

For example, in each of these sentences the word 'round' belongs to a different class.

He looked through the round window.

She ran round the block.

The sheepdog began to round up the flock.

The ladies played a round of golf.

IN THE CLASSROOM

OPEN AND CLOSED WORD CLASSES

Some word classes can be said to be 'open' because we constantly add words to them. For example, new nouns are regularly added to the dictionary as we need to name new inventions or ideas or as we acquire different ways of naming things from other countries, both English-speaking and non-English-speaking. Think of a menu in an Italian restaurant where you might find pizza, spaghetti, pasta, ciabatta and so on. None of these words was in common use in England 100 years ago, but now most people know what they mean. We've acquired new words in information technology such as email, USB, laptop and memory stick.

Similarly, we are constantly acquiring new verbs. In the London Olympics, we heard of people 'medalling' when they won an event. Social media have given us a whole new vocabulary, including such verbs as 'tweet', 'unfriend' and 'blog'.

To find out more about new words, see **http://blog.oxforddictionaries.com/2013/08/new-words-august-2013/**

CLASSROOM ACTIVITIES

NONSENSE SENTENCES

This activity encourages children to discuss the roles of words in sentences and enables you and them to make use of correct terminology.

RESOURCES

Examples of nonsense sentences (for a lesson plan and examples, see Waugh and McGuinn, 1996). Make up a series of examples. The following might get you started:

The silly badger phoned the wooden balloon.

A tiny elephant rode a purple banana.

WHAT TO DO

Write a nonsense sentence on the board and read it to the children. Explain that you want them to work in pairs to write their own nonsense sentences and that you don't want any sensible sentences. Their sentences must follow the pattern of yours exactly, so for the first example above they would need: determiner ('the'), adjective ('silly'), common noun ('badger'), verb ('phoned'), determiner ('the'), adjective ('wooden') and common noun ('balloon'). When they share their sentences, discuss the structures and ask others to say if they accurately follow the pattern. This is the time to discuss word classes and to ask if the children used the terms in their discussions.

Continue the activity using different structures, perhaps introducing adverbs, prepositions, pronouns and conjunctions.

SONG AND BOOK TITLES

A whole-class game or group activity that draws upon popular culture to focus children's attention on word classes.

RESOURCES

Either on a computer or on pieces of paper, write the names of book titles and songs that the children know (e.g. *Charlie and the Chocolate Factory*, *Matilda*, 'Ten Green Bottles', 'White Christmas').

WHAT TO DO

After discussing word classes, show groups of titles next to each other and ask the children to identify the title you are describing. For example, if you used four Beatles songs ('From Me to You', 'Twist and Shout', 'Get Back' and 'Fool on the Hill'), you could ask the children to identify each with statements such as:

Preposition-pronoun-preposition-pronoun

Verb-conjunction-verb

Verb-preposition

Noun-preposition-determiner-noun

The children can go on to find other titles and give each other clues to identify them.

For more information on word classes, see **www.ucl.ac.uk/internet-grammar/wordclas/wordclas.htm**

REFERENCES

DfE (2013) *The National Curriculum*. London: DfE.

Waugh, D. and McGuinn, N. (1996) *Writing KS2 (Curriculum Bank)*. Leamington Spa: Scholastic.

FURTHER READING

Waugh, D., Warner, C. and Waugh, R. (2019) *Teaching Grammar, Punctuation and Spelling in Primary Schools* (3rd edition). London: SAGE.

10

NOUNS

WHAT DO I NEED TO KNOW?

A noun is a word used to name a person, animal, place, thing or abstract idea. The English word 'noun' comes from the Latin *nōmen*, meaning 'name' or 'noun'. Think about some of the words we use in English that come from this: 'nominate', 'nominal', 'nomenclature'.

There are different types of nouns, including proper, common and abstract.

PROPER NOUN

A proper noun is a name for something unique such as a place, person, day of the week, month or product, so the following are proper nouns: 'Doncaster', 'Nelson Mandela', 'Wednesday', 'October' and 'Toyota'.

COMMON NOUN

Common nouns are the words for people, places, animals and things, but they are not the *actual* names of people, places or things.

ABSTRACT NOUN

An abstract noun can be an idea, experience, concept, state of being, trait, quality, feeling or anything else we cannot experience using our senses. These include emotions and feelings such as love, hatred, fear, joy, pride and happiness; attributes such as loyalty, honesty, courage and compassion; and ideas, concepts and ideals such as truth, knowledge, justice, dedication and faith. Some curricula and grammar texts apply the term 'concrete nouns' to all of those nouns that are not abstract.

Nouns with the suffixes below are often abstract. An example is provided for each. Can you think of further examples?

-tion	elation
-ism	professionalism
-age	usage
-ance	performance
-ity	ability
-ship	relationship
-ability	disability
-acy	privacy
-ment	excitement
-ness	happiness
-ence	preference

If you are unsure whether a word is a noun, try putting an article such as 'a', 'an' or 'the' in front of it. If it sounds right without adding other words, you almost certainly have a noun (e.g. 'a friendship', 'a chocolate', 'an apple', 'the bicycle', 'a performance').

WHAT IS IT USEFUL TO KNOW?

WHY ARE NOUNS USEFUL?

Our earliest forms of communication as babies or as users of a foreign language usually involve nouns. We have a desire to be able to name things and to tell people what we want. So, a baby who is just learning her first few words will quickly learn 'mummy', 'daddy', 'cup', 'teddy' and so on, while a traveller in a country where he cannot speak the language will need to know a basic vocabulary of nouns for eating, finding accommodation and directions.

Almost all common or concrete nouns can be modified to show that there is more than one of something (see also Chapter 6). Usually, this involves adding an '-s' as in all but one of the examples above, but sometimes '-es' is added and sometimes words remain the same in the plural or change in other ways. 'Teeth', for example, is the plural of 'tooth'.

COUNT AND NON-COUNT NOUNS

COUNT NOUNS

Those nouns that can become plural are often referred to as count nouns. We can have one cake, or two, three or many cakes. Count nouns can be singular or plural (e.g. 'book', 'dog', 'watch' and 'mouse' can become 'books', 'dogs', 'watches' and 'mice').

We can use the determiner 'a'/'an' with count nouns:

A horse is an animal.

When a count noun is singular, we must use a word such as 'a'/'the'/'my'/'this' with it:

I want <u>an</u> orange. (<u>not</u> I want orange.)

Where is <u>my</u> bottle? (<u>not</u> Where is bottle?)

When a count noun is plural, we can use it alone:

I like oranges.

Bottles can break.

We can use 'some' and 'any' with count nouns:

I have <u>some</u> chocolates.

Do you have <u>any</u> sweets?

We can use 'a few' and 'many' with count nouns:

I have <u>a few</u> chocolates.

I don't have <u>many</u> sweets.

NON-COUNT NOUNS

Non-count nouns are substances, concepts and so on that we cannot divide into separate elements. We cannot 'count' them. For example, we cannot count sugar, but we can count bags of sugar or spoonfuls of sugar. Non-count nouns include 'music', 'happiness', 'advice', 'information', 'news', 'furniture', 'sugar', 'behaviour' and 'electricity'.

We usually treat non-count nouns as singular. We use a singular verb. For example:

This <u>news is</u> very important.

Your <u>luggage looks</u> heavy.

Sometimes the same noun can be count *and* non-count, often with a change of meaning. So, we might use 'time' in two different ways:

I have watched Rovers more than a thousand times.

I don't have time to watch football any more.

When we want to use the words 'less' or 'fewer', we decide which is appropriate by deciding if the noun is count or non-count.

If it is count, we use 'fewer':

I have seen Rovers fewer times this year than last.

If it is non-count, we use 'less':

I have less time than I used to have.

COLLECTIVE NOUNS

The English language includes hundreds of collective nouns that all mean 'a group' but are different according to the type of group. So, we have 'a murder of crows', 'a flock of geese', 'a herd of elephants', 'a gaggle of geese', 'an exaltation of larks' and 'a litter of pigs'. Besides the established collective nouns, there are others that people invent (something children might enjoy doing) that can be found online. For a host of examples, see **www.ojohaven.com/collectives/index. html#footnote** and **www.rinkworks.com/words/collective.shtml**

KEY KNOWLEDGE SUMMARY

Nouns are the words that identify things, people, ideas or feelings. The names of specific people, places or things are called *proper nouns* and are written with capital letters at the start. Nouns referring to intangible ideas or feelings are called *abstract nouns*. Most nouns can be made into a plural form, but those referring to something that cannot be counted do not have plural forms.

IN THE CLASSROOM

Nouns are usually the first words children learn, and the first words adults learn when visiting a foreign country. We go on to link them to verbs and adjectives – 'drink milk', 'eat cake', 'red shoes', 'big dog' and so on.

Most curricula require children to be able to name things in different subjects. For example, in England's science curriculum (DfE, 2013), Year 1 children are expected to do the following:

- become familiar with the common names of birds, fish, amphibians, reptiles, mammals and invertebrates, including pets; and

- have plenty of opportunities to learn the names of the main body parts (including head, neck, arms, elbows, legs, knees, face, ears, eyes, hair, mouth, teeth) through games, actions, songs and rhymes.

As children develop their understanding of language, they will see that many nouns can also be used as verbs or adjectives. For example, 'love' is an abstract noun in the first sentence below and a verb in the second:

Love is all you need to be happy.

I love chips.

Sometimes we change nouns into verbs by adding a suffix (see Chapter 6). This often leads to new words being invented and sometimes to angry letters to newspapers decrying falling standards – the use of 'medalled' and 'podiumed' at the London Olympics to indicate that someone had won a medal and had stood on the winners' podium induced considerable wrath in some quarters! However, we have always done this with nouns, and Shakespeare was a major 'culprit'.

RESOURCES

It can be useful to create a table or chart of different types of nouns as a reference point in the classroom. You might also pose the question: Which of the nouns in the chart can belong to different word classes depending on how we use them?

GENDER AND NOUNS

Generally, in English, nouns do not have different genders, but some words are modified slightly in the feminine form, usually because they come from French. For example, usually 'blond' has an 'e' at the end when it refers to a female's hair, but not for a male; a fiancé is a man, but a fiancée is a woman.

NOUN PHRASES

A noun phrase is a group of words built up round a single noun, which is called the headword of the phrase. So, we can have the following:

A brown dog bit me.

Some children were playing cricket.

The man who came to see me yesterday is here again.

As children develop their understanding of nouns, they learn to use adjectives and phrases to add precision. You can encourage this through shared writing by inviting children to help you to make a passage more interesting by creating noun phrases.

CLASSROOM ACTIVITIES

SETS AND SUBSETS

A simple activity to help children to see the difference between common and proper nouns, and to help them to understand that things can be part of sets and subsets.

RESOURCES

Dictionaries and internet access.

WHAT TO DO

Explain that we use sets and subsets to classify nouns with increasing precision For example, start with a general term on the board (e.g. 'animals'). Show how this can include subsets such as 'fish', 'birds' and 'dogs'. Ask the children for their suggestions. Then show how each of these subsets can be further divided. 'Dogs' can include 'Labradors', 'sheepdogs', 'poodles' and 'terriers' – the children will be keen to suggest more, and can use dictionaries to check spellings. This can be a useful vocabulary exercise in an EAL context as well.

COLLECTING AND CLASSIFYING NOUNS

A simple activity that focuses attention on different forms and types of nouns.

RESOURCES

A range of texts.

WHAT TO DO

In shared and individual reading, ask the children to look for nouns to classify under the following headings:

- Collective nouns

- Nouns always expressed in the plural

- Nouns that are the same in both singular and plural

- '-s' and '-es' endings

- Irregular forms

MAKING NOUN POEMS

A creative activity that involves looking at abstract nouns and creating simple poems.

RESOURCES

Board and list of abstract nouns.

WHAT TO DO

Show the children a series of pictures that display a range of emotions, or a short video clip of, say, a race at the Olympic Games. Ask them to think of different abstract nouns to name the emotions they see. Help them by providing a list of abstract nouns, but encourage them to share their own ideas. One Year 5 class produced the following after watching the final of the 100-metre race:

excitement

tension

anticipation

action

acceleration

exhilaration

celebration

REFERENCE

DfE (2013) *The National Curriculum*. London: DfE, pp144–75.

FURTHER READING

Waugh, D., Warner, C. and Waugh, R. (2019) *Teaching Grammar, Punctuation and Spelling in Primary Schools* (3rd edition). London: SAGE, Chapter 2.

USEFUL WEBSITE

For more information about word class/parts of speech, see **www.writingcentre.uottawa.ca/ hypergrammar/nouns.html**

11

VERBS

WHAT DO I NEED TO KNOW?

A verb is a word that shows an action or state of being. Whatever you are doing can be expressed by a verb.

Every sentence must have a verb in it. A sentence can have only one word, as long as the word is a verb:

Jump!

Stop!

Shoot!

Exclamations such as 'Oh dear!' and 'Oh! What a brilliant goal!' are not sentences because they do not have verbs.

The three principal parts of verbs are *present*, *past* and *past participle*. The present is used by itself for the present tense:

I run.

I laugh.

An auxiliary (helping) verb 'will' or 'shall' is added for the future tense:

I will run.

I will laugh.

Verbs usually change for the past tense. Often '-ed' is added for the past tense, but sometimes other parts of the word change:

I ran.

I laughed.

The past participle is used with the verb 'have' ('has', 'had') to form perfect tenses.

Present perfect:

> *I have <u>jumped</u>.*
>
> *I have <u>eaten</u>.*

Past perfect:

> *I had <u>jumped</u>.*
>
> *I had <u>eaten</u>.*

Future perfect:

> *I will <u>have jumped</u>.*
>
> *I will <u>have eaten</u>.*

FUTURE

Although many languages have a different form for verbs when talking about the future, English verbs do not have a future tense: we talk about the future by using modal verbs with the present tense form. For example:

> *Today I read the paper: tomorrow <u>I am going to</u> read the paper, or I <u>shall</u> read the paper.*
>
> *Yesterday David walked five miles: tomorrow he <u>is going to</u> walk seven, or he <u>will</u> walk seven.*

WHAT IS IT USEFUL TO KNOW?

IMPERATIVE VERBS

Imperative verbs give an order or instruction:

> *Sit down!*
>
> *Eat your greens!*

ADDING PREFIXES TO VERBS

Many verbs can have their meanings changed or modified by using prefixes such as 'dis-', 're-' or 'over-'. For example:

> *to dislike*
>
> *to reclaim*
>
> *to overcharge*

PROGRESSIVE FORMS OF VERBS

These are often called continuous or imperfect forms; the term is used when the action of the verb has been going on for a while, rather than being one specific completed action. They all include a present participle (the '-ing' form). For example:

I had been working in the garden.

The children were eating their lunch.

James will have been teaching for three years next month.

THE PRESENT PERFECT FORM OF VERBS

This refers to an action that has happened once and been completed:

He has read this book.

We have finished our work.

STANDARD AND NON-STANDARD USE OF VERBS

In many dialects, non-standard forms of verbs are used. This applies, in particular, to the verb 'to be', so that in some areas many people might say 'we was' and 'you was' rather than 'we were' or 'you were', or 'I ain't' rather than 'I'm not'.

Young children often make mistakes when they begin to speak and write. Sometimes this is because of the language they hear around them and sometimes it occurs because they apply a rule they know (usually unconsciously) inappropriately. So, a frequent mistake is for children to add '-ed' to verbs in the past tense even when the verbs are irregular and do not need the '-ed' suffix. For example, you will almost certainly encounter some of the following: 'I goed', 'we wented', 'I catched it' and 'we buyed it'.

CONVERTING NOUNS OR ADJECTIVES INTO VERBS USING SUFFIXES (SEE CHAPTER 6)

It is quite common for new verbs to be created from other parts of speech by using the suffixes '-ify' or '-itise'. Children can enjoy experimenting with these, creating their own new verbs. There is also an increasing tendency, however, simply to use nouns as verbs, as was frequently noticed at sports events with the constant use of 'medalled' to mean 'awarded a medal'. We also do this in 'to text', 'to email' and 'to action something'.

MODAL VERBS

This term refers to the verbs that in English form part of some tenses, such as 'should', 'would', 'could', 'will', 'can', 'have', 'may', 'might' and so on.

Modal verbs behave differently from normal verbs.

1. MODAL VERBS DO NOT ADD '-S' IN THE THIRD PERSON

For example:

> *She can play chess.*
>
> *He should wash his car.*

Compare with:

> *She plays chess.*
>
> *He washes his car.*

2. 'NOT' IS USED TO MAKE MODAL VERBS NEGATIVE, EVEN IN SIMPLE PRESENT AND SIMPLE PAST

For example:

> *She should not drive so quickly.*
>
> *We might not go on holiday.*

3. MANY MODAL VERBS CANNOT BE USED IN PAST TENSES OR FUTURE TENSES

For example:

> Sarah will can ride a bike. *incorrect*
>
> He musted change trains at Crewe. *incorrect*

REGULAR AND IRREGULAR VERBS

Most verbs in English follow a regular pattern, as noted above; the exceptions are mostly fairly common words, though unpredictable. New words coming into the language are nearly always assimilated into the regular pattern of a past in '-ed'.

KEY KNOWLEDGE SUMMARY

Verbs are the words that tell you what is happening in a sentence . One verb on its own can be a sentence, and a group of words without a verb is not a sentence. Verbs usually change their form when referring to the past and use auxiliary ('helping') or modal verbs to create forms for talking about the future. Many verbs in English follow a regular pattern, but a lot of common examples need to be learnt on an individual basis.

IN THE CLASSROOM

The English National Curriculum (DfE, 2013) refers to verbs for Years 1–5.

YEAR	REFERENCE TO VERBS
1	*Suffixes* that can be added to *verbs* where no change is needed in the spelling of root words (e.g. *helping, helped, helper*).
	How the *prefix un-* changes the meaning of *verbs* and *adjectives* (negation, *e.g. unkind*, or undoing, *e.g. untie the boat*).
2	Use of the *progressive* form of *verbs* in the *present* and *past tense* to mark actions in progress (e.g. *she is drumming, he was shouting*).
3	Use of the *present perfect* form of *verbs* instead of the simple past (e.g. *He has gone out to play* contrasted with *He went out to play*).
4	Standard English forms for *verb inflections* instead of local spoken forms (e.g. *we were* instead of *we was*, or *I did* instead of *I done*).
5	Converting *nouns* or *adjectives* into *verbs* using *suffixes* (e.g. *-ate; -ise; -ify*).
	Verb prefixes (e.g. *dis-, de-, mis-, over-* and *re-*).
	Indicating degrees of possibility using *adverbs* (e.g. *perhaps, surely*) or *modal verbs* (e.g. *might, should, will, must*).

The verb 'to be' is the most used verb in the English language.

The verb 'to be' uses eight words to express the standard forms: 'am', 'are', 'is', 'was', 'were', 'be', 'being' and 'been'.

PRESENT TENSE	PAST TENSE	FUTURE TENSE	PRESENT PERFECT TENSE	PAST PERFECT TENSE	FUTURE PERFECT TENSE
I *am*	I *was*	I will *be*	I have *been*	I had *been*	I will have *been*
you *are*	you *were*	you will *be*	you have *been*	you had *been*	you will have *been*
he/she/it *is*	he/she/it *was*	he/she/it will *be*	he/she/it has *been*	he/she/it had *been*	he/she/it will have *been*
we *are*	we *were*	we will *be*	we have *been*	we had *been*	we will have *been*
they *are*	they *were*	they will *be*	they have *been*	they had *been*	they will have *been*

In the future forms, it can also be correct to say 'I shall' and 'we shall'.

WHAT DO WE MEAN BY PERFECT AND IMPERFECT TENSES?

The perfect tense is used for referring to an action that happened once and was then finished:

James fell over.

I finished reading my book.

The imperfect tense is for referring to an action that either went on for a long time, was repeated or was interrupted. Many languages have a specific form for this usage. In English, it is usually either 'was … "-ing"' or 'used to':

While he was eating his lunch, a letter arrived.

When I was little, I used to live in the countryside.

CLASSROOM ACTIVITIES
LOOKING FOR ALTERNATIVE VERBS

An activity that encourages children to think about alternatives to common verbs.

RESOURCES

Use a thesaurus to find alternatives to commonly used verbs. Prepare by writing some of these words in the centre of sheets of paper, circling them and leaving space for the children to write alternatives of synonyms around them.

For example, you might use:

ran – jogged, sprinted, galloped, dashed

ate – munched, gobbled, chomped, chewed, guzzled

hit – biffed, thumped, bashed, bopped

said – whispered, cried, shouted, muttered

WHAT TO DO

Begin by reading a short passage of dialogue to the children. Explain that there are several different words that can be used instead of 'said' and read the passage again, asking the children to spot these.

Now ask the children to look at storybooks that include dialogue to see how many variations they can find on 'said'. Give them the sheets with 'said' in the middle and ask them to write as many alternatives as possible around the word.

Next, ask the children to look at other verbs to see how many alternatives they can find. They can do this through discussion first, but later they may use a dictionary or thesaurus.

In subsequent lessons, ask the children to draw upon their findings to vary vocabulary in their writing.

Make collections of interesting verbs using stories, poems and newspapers.

CHANGING TENSES

A simple activity that encourages children to think about the past forms of verbs.

RESOURCES

Make a collection of verbs that the children are likely to meet in the next few weeks. Write these on cards and display them. Provide some blank cards on which the past tenses of the verbs can be written.

WHAT TO DO

Say some verbs (e.g. 'run', 'ask', 'play', 'sleep', 'read', 'catch', 'go', 'see') and ask the children to discuss the past tense versions.

Discuss the irregular past tenses for 'run' ('ran'), 'read' ('read'), 'catch' ('caught') and 'see' ('saw'), and compare these words with others that add '-ed' in the past tense.

Ask the children to find examples of verbs in the past tense in various texts. Get them to list these under the headings 'irregular' and 'regular' and discuss which type occurs most often.

REFERENCE

DfE (2013) *The National Curriculum*. London: DfE.

FURTHER READING

Waugh, D., Warner, C. and Waugh, R. (2019) *Teaching Grammar, Punctuation and Spelling in Primary Schools* (3rd edition). London: SAGE, Chapter 2.

12

ADJECTIVES

WHAT DO I NEED TO KNOW?

WHAT IS AN ADJECTIVE?

Adjectives qualify, or tell us more about, nouns by answering one of these three questions:

1. What kind is it?

2. How many are there?

3. Which one is it?

They are sometimes called 'describing words', although this is not helpful as other types of words such as adverbs are also used to describe. Determiners such as 'a', 'an' or 'the' are also generally considered as adjectives, because they tell us whether there is a particular object being referred to.

The work of an adjective can be done by a single word, a phrase or a clause:

The house was <u>enormous</u>.

The house was <u>near the forest</u>.

He loved the house <u>that he had inherited</u>.

Adjectives often precede nouns:

an enormous house

a lovely view

a red car

Sometimes it may be more effective to use a more precise noun rather than use an adjective (e.g. 'mansion' instead of 'big house').

Avoid repeating adjectives, unless to gain a specific effect, as in, for example, the traditional story-telling formula:

In a dark, dark wood stood a dark, dark house …

WHAT IS IT USEFUL TO KNOW?

Both ordinal and cardinal numbers are adjectives:

The fourth book was the longest.

In front of the bank stood three cars.

Many words can be used as either adjectives or adverbs:

He played <u>well</u> *(adverb – tells us how he played)*

He is not <u>well</u> *(adjective – describes him)*

My friend runs <u>fast</u> *(adverb – tells us how he runs)*

We caught a <u>fast</u> train *(adjective – describes the train)*

We can form adjectives by adding suffixes (see Chapter 6) to nouns (e.g. abstract nouns):

beauty *becomes* beautiful

hope *becomes* hopeless

love *becomes* lovely

COMPARATIVE AND SUPERLATIVE ADJECTIVES

When we compare two people or things, we tend to use the word 'than' between the adjective and the noun:

Jamie was taller than Dean.

Sian was fitter than William.

When we compare three or more things, we tend to use 'the' before the superlative adjective:

Jamie was the tallest in the class.

Messi is the best player in the world.

The suffixes '-er' and '-est' are used to form most comparatives and superlatives, although we need '-ier' and '-iest' when a two-syllable adjective ends in '-y' ('lovely' and 'loveliest', 'lazy' and 'laziest'). Otherwise, we use more and most when an adjective has more than one syllable:

Italy is even more beautiful than Wales.

It is the most beautiful country in Europe.

Some adjectives are irregular in their comparative and superlative forms, so we do not say 'bad', 'badder', 'baddest'; we say 'bad', 'worse', 'worst'.

Some irregular comparative and superlative adjectives are shown in the table below.

POSITIVE	COMPARATIVE	SUPERLATIVE
good	better	best
bad	worse	worst
far	further	furthest
little	less	least
much many some	more	most

Two comparative and superlative forms that are often confused are 'less'/'least' and 'fewer'/'fewest'. 'Fewer'/'fewest' should be used when the noun is a 'count noun' (something measured in whole numbers):

Scotland has fewer cities than England.

'Less'/'least' should be used if the quantity is not measured in units:

I have less money than you.

This is the least attractive room.

When an adjective is formed from a proper noun, it should be capitalised. Thus, we write about 'Christian music', 'French polish', 'the British Parliament', 'the Ming dynasty', 'a Dickensian style' and 'Athenian democracy'. Some periods of time have taken on the status of proper adjectives (e.g. 'the Victorian era', 'a Renaissance poet').

KEY KNOWLEDGE SUMMARY

WHAT IS AN ADJECTIVE?

A word that tells us more about a noun in a sentence or phrase. Adjectives are single words; adjectival phrases or clauses can do the same job. Most adjectives have three forms: simple, comparative and superlative.

WHAT IS THE DIFFERENCE BETWEEN 'LESS' AND 'FEWER'?

We use 'fewer' for count nouns and 'less' for undefined quantities – 'fewer minutes', but 'less time'!

IN THE CLASSROOM

In the English National Curriculum (DfE, 2013), children first learn about adjectives in Year 1, although most will have used adjectives in their speech before coming to school. When you next hear young children talking, notice how they use adjectives to specify what they want: 'a red one', 'a new one' and so on.

YEAR 1

How the prefix 'un-' changes the meaning of verbs and adjectives (negation, e.g. 'unkind', or undoing, e.g. 'untie the boat').

YEAR 2

Formation of adjectives using suffixes such as '-ful' and '-less'.

YEAR 4

Noun phrases expanded by the addition of modifying adjectives, nouns and preposition phrases (e.g. 'the teacher' expanded to 'the strict maths teacher with curly hair').

There can be a tendency to overuse adjectives. Used sparingly, adjectives enhance writing by adding description. However, if we use too many, we may not engage our readers.

Look at examples of high-quality writing for children, such as books by Michael Morpurgo and Roald Dahl, and you will see that the authors are rather more sparing in their use of adjectives, but still manage to describe people and things very effectively. When discussing adjectives with children, it is a good idea to look at examples from well-known authors.

WHERE DO WE PLACE ADJECTIVES?

In English, most adjectives are placed *before* a noun:

> It was a *lovely day*.

> I read a very *interesting book* yesterday.

Or *after a link verb* such as 'be', 'look' or 'feel':

> The day was *lovely*.

> The book seems *interesting*.

FORMING ADJECTIVES WITH PREFIXES

A range of prefixes, mostly from Latin or Greek, can be used to alter or modify adjectives. Children can experiment with using them. The list could include:

dis-	*not*	*dissatisfied*
intra-	*inside*	*intravenous*
trans-	*across*	*transworld*
sub-	*under*	*subconscious*
super-	*over*	*supernumerary*
un-	*not*	*unwanted*

FORMING ADJECTIVES WITH SUFFIXES (SEE ALSO CHAPTER 6)

Suffixes such as '-ish', '-like' or '-able' can change other parts of speech into adjectives. Again, children can enjoy seeing how many ways they can find, as well as creating new words.

DIFFERENT TYPES OF ADJECTIVES

Although an adjective is often defined as a 'describing word', some groups of words do not quite fit into this category. They are, however, still adjectives because their role is to tell us more about a noun. Numbers, for instance, are an example that has already been mentioned. Other examples include:

- *Articles*: the definite article ('the') and the indefinite article ('a'/'an'/'some') tell the reader whether a specific article is being referred to.

- *Possessive adjectives*: 'my'/'mine', 'your'/'yours', 'his', 'her'/'hers', 'our'/'ours', 'their'/'theirs':

  His house is bigger than mine.

  Are those books all yours?

- *Demonstrative adjectives*: 'this', 'these', 'that'. These tell us more about a noun by indicating that a specific thing is being referred to:

  I like this coat more than that.

  We enjoyed those sandwiches.

- *Indefinite adjectives*: words that refer to a quantity of something (e.g. 'many', 'most', 'few', 'several', 'no'):

  James saw no badgers, but his friend spotted several.

- *Personal titles*: 'Mrs', 'Dr', 'Lord', when followed by a name.

CLASSROOM ACTIVITIES

The activities below may be developed into lessons or may form parts of lessons.

CREATE A LIST OF INTERESTING ADJECTIVES EACH TIME YOU ASK CHILDREN TO PRODUCE DESCRIPTIVE WRITING

When discussing a writing activity with the children, invite them to suggest adjectives that might be appropriate for describing different characters, events or places. List these on the board or make a quick display so that the children can draw upon these as they write. Remember to discourage them from using too many adjectives at once.

CHANGE ADJECTIVES IN A PIECE OF TEXT

Work in pairs or small groups to discuss possibilities.

Provide examples of text in which all of the descriptions involve a limited range of adjectives such as 'nice', 'good' and 'happy'. Ask the children to change the adjectives to enhance the writing and make it more interesting.

COMPARATIVE ADJECTIVES LESSON LINKED TO MATHS

Look at adjectives that compare mass, length and capacity. Talk with the children about the forms we use when comparing two items (e.g. 'longer', 'heavier', 'shorter', 'lighter') and the forms used when comparing three or more items (e.g. 'longest', 'heaviest', 'shortest', 'lightest').

MAKE CHARTS OF ADJECTIVE SYNONYMS AND ANTONYMS

Take words such as 'nice' and ask the children to suggest alternatives for different situations (e.g. 'delicious', 'tasty', 'succulent' for food; 'pleasant', 'friendly', 'kind' for people). Make charts of synonymous adjectives to display and act as a resource when the children are writing.

Go on to make charts of antonym adjectives such as 'good'/'bad', 'happy'/'sad' and 'high'/'low' (see Chapter 18).

REFERENCE

DfE (2013) *The National Curriculum*. London: DfE.

FURTHER READING

Waugh, D., Warner, C. and Waugh, R. (2019) *Teaching Grammar, Punctuation and Spelling in Primary Schools* (3rd edition). London: SAGE, Chapter 2.

USEFUL WEBSITES

For more information about adjectives, see **www.chompchomp.com/terms/adjective.htm**

For a list of over 1,000 adjectives, see **www.momswhothink.com/reading/list-of-adjectives. html#Adjectives List**

13

ADVERBS

WHAT DO I NEED TO KNOW?

Adverbs are used to modify a verb, an adjective, or another adverb:

Mo runs quickly.

Toby is an extremely intelligent boy.

The train goes incredibly fast.

In the first example, the adverb 'quickly' tells us how Mo runs. In the second example, the adverb 'extremely' tells us the degree to which Toby is intelligent. In the third example, the adverb 'incredibly' tells us how fast the train goes.

CHARACTERISTICS OF ADVERBS

'-LY' ADVERBS

Many adverbs end in '-ly': they are formed by adding '-ly' to an adjective:

adjective	rough	quick	nice	sudden	pretty
adverb	roughly	quickly	nicely	suddenly	prettily

These adverbs are known as '-ly' adverbs. However, not all adverbs end in '-ly', and you should not assume that all words that end in '-ly' are adverbs.

Some adjectives also end in '-ly', including 'heavenly', 'friendly', 'likely', 'lovely', 'manly' and 'timely'. Try creating sentences that include each of these adjectives. You will find that they cannot be used to modify verbs, except in some dialects or in common but incorrect usage. For example, 'This car goes lovely' would be incorrect, but 'This is a lovely car' would be correct, and 'lovely' is an adjective that describes it.

Look at these sentences and decide which of the underlined words are adjectives and which are adverbs:

Stupidly, I left my wallet in the pub.

Boris is a lively character.

Sara's father was a friendly person.

Ed slowly discovered the truth.

The first and fourth examples are adverbs because 'stupidly' describes the way in which I left (a verb) my wallet, and 'slowly' describes how Ed discovered (a verb) the truth. In the second example, 'lively' describes Boris's character (a noun), and so is an adjective, while in the third example 'friendly' describes the noun 'person', and so is an adjective.

GRADABLE ADVERBS

Many adverbs, like many adjectives, are *gradable*: we can use words such as 'very', 'extremely' and 'incredibly' to modify them:

quickly	very quickly
hastily	extremely hastily
slowly	incredibly slowly
stupidly	quite stupidly
noisily	rather noisily

DEGREE ADVERBS

Words such as 'very', 'incredibly' and 'extremely' are *degree adverbs*. Degree adverbs tell us the extent or degree to which an adjective or another adverb applies. The list below shows a selection of degree adverbs (see **www.englishclub.com/vocabulary/adverbs-degree.htm**):

absolutely	extremely	just	pretty	terribly
almost	fairly	least	purely	thoroughly
awfully	far	less	quite	too
badly	fully	little	rather	totally
barely	greatly	lots	really	utterly
completely	hardly	most	scarcely	very
decidedly	highly	much	simply	virtually
deeply	how	nearly	so	well
enormously	incredibly	perfectly	somewhat	
enough	indeed	positively	strongly	
entirely	intensely	practically		

Degree adverbs cannot usually be gradable, although we do sometimes use words such as 'very', 'extremely' and 'incredibly' with some of them. For example:

The crime was extremely thoroughly investigated.

He finished very strongly.

City played incredibly badly.

COMPARATIVE AND SUPERLATIVE ADVERBS

Look at the words 'hard', 'harder' and 'hardest' in the sentences below:

It was hard work.

It was harder work than usual.

It was the hardest work I've ever done.

In each sentence, 'hard' is an adjective (see Chapter 12) because it describes a noun, 'work'. Now look at the sentences below:

I work hard every day.

I work harder than I used to.

I work hardest when there is a deadline.

In each of these sentences, 'hard' is an adverb because it modifies the verb 'work'. So, 'work' can be both a noun and a verb, depending on how it is used, and 'hard' can be an adjective when it describes something and an adverb when it describes how something was done. In the examples above, you can see that 'hard' can be modified by adding '-er' when we compare two things and by adding '-est'. For most adverbs, comparatives and superlatives are created by using 'more' and 'most'.

ADVERB	COMPARATIVE	SUPERLATIVE
slowly	more slowly	most slowly
creatively	more creatively	most creatively
regularly	more regularly	most regularly
rapidly	more rapidly	most rapidly

Some adverbs are irregular in their comparative and superlative forms, and these often lead to errors for young children and people learning English as an additional language. How often have you heard children use words such as 'bestest'?

ADVERB	COMPARATIVE	SUPERLATIVE
do well	do better	do the best
run badly	run worse	run the worst

| spend little | spend less | spend the least |
| eat much | eat more | eat the most |

See **www.ucl.ac.uk/internet-grammar/adverbs/adverbs.htm**

WHAT IS IT USEFUL TO KNOW?

CIRCUMSTANTIAL ADVERBS: TIME, MANNER AND PLACE

Many adverbs tell us about the time, manner or place of an event or action. They tell us:

- when an action occurs/occurred or how frequently (time);

- how an action occurred (manner); or

- where an action occurred (place).

Examples are provided below of adverbs of time, adverbs of manner and adverbs of place.

Adverbs of time:

I'll do it <u>tomorrow</u>.

I <u>still</u> haven't been given a knighthood.

She <u>always</u> chews gum.

Adverbs of manner:

He drove the car <u>dangerously</u>.

<u>Nervously</u>, she stroked the fierce dog.

She <u>easily</u> beat her nearest rival in the race.

Adverbs of place:

She drove <u>there</u>.

I was finally getting <u>somewhere</u>.

<u>Near the house</u> was a large forest.

KEY KNOWLEDGE SUMMARY

Adverbs tell us how, in what way, when, where, and to what extent the action of a verb happens. An adverb may be a single word, and many of these end in '-ly'. A phrase that does this job is called an adverbial phrase, and when this is placed at the beginning of a sentence it is a 'fronted adverbial'.

Many adverbs are gradable and can be used with another adverb to show degree (e.g. 'very quickly', 'fairly quickly').

IN THE CLASSROOM

Children begin to use adverbs before they start school. The English National Curriculum (DfE, 2013) requires children to understand how to use adverbs in different ways:

YEAR	DETAIL
2	Use of the suffixes '-er', '-est' in adjectives and '-ly' to turn adjectives into adverbs.
3	Expressing time, place and cause using conjunctions (e.g. 'when', 'before', 'after', 'while', 'so', 'because'), adverbs (e.g. 'then', 'next', 'soon', 'therefore') or prepositions (e.g. 'before', 'after', 'during', 'in', 'because of').
5	Indicating degrees of possibility using adverbs (e.g. 'perhaps', 'surely') or modal verbs (e.g. 'might', 'should', 'will', 'must').

The curriculum also refers to adverbials, which are phrases that act in the same way as single-word adverbs to tell us more about how actions are performed and so on.

YEAR	DETAIL
4	Fronted adverbials (e.g. *Later that day*, I heard the bad news'). Use of commas after fronted adverbials.
5	Linking ideas across paragraphs using adverbials of time (e.g. 'later'), place (e.g. 'nearby') and number (e.g. 'secondly').
6	Linking ideas across paragraphs using a wider range of cohesive devices: repetition of a word or phrase, grammatical connections (e.g. the use of adverbials such as 'on the other hand', 'in contrast' or 'as a consequence') and ellipsis.

FRONTED ADVERBIALS

In English, we can often be flexible about word order in sentences. For example:

I went to the cinema when I had finished work.

This could be presented as:

When I had finished work, I went to the cinema.

By moving adverbs and adverbial phrases to the beginning of sentences occasionally, we can vary our writing and make it more interesting for readers.

CHILDREN'S MISCONCEPTIONS

The adverb that corresponds to the adjective 'good' is 'well', so the sentences below are incorrect:

John played really good.

I'm doing good.

Children often use 'good' as an adverb when 'well' would be correct, although you will rarely hear anyone make the mistake of turning 'good' into 'goodly' as an adverb ('goodly' is a rather antiquated adjective – 'a goodly helping'). One of the reasons for the misuse of 'good' rather than 'well' is US television and films, in which characters often respond to questions such as 'How are you?' with answers such as 'I'm doing good' or 'I'm good, thanks'. Sports commentators also often say that a player has 'done good' instead of 'done well'. Of course, it would be correct to say 'I'm doing good' if you meant to say that you were bringing benefits to other people. And if you were profiting from this, you could be 'doing well by doing good'!

The same process of using adjectives instead of adverbs is extending to other words as well in advertising slogans – 'eat healthy', 'think clever', 'shop smart' – and the trend seems likely to continue, perhaps because the adjective is shorter and 'punchier'. It is important, though, for children to understand that they should not use this type of construction in formal writing.

Although many adverbs end with '-ly', it is wrong to say that an adverb must end in '-ly'. There are many common adverbs without an '-ly' ending such as 'tomorrow', 'yesterday', 'always', 'soon' and 'almost'.

CLASSROOM ACTIVITIES

ADVERBS IN PE

Simple activities to emphasise the nature of adverbs in a kinaesthetic way.

RESOURCES

None apart from a hall or playground.

WHAT TO DO

Ask the children to produce a sequence of three movements related to the same verb (e.g. 'run slowly', 'run quickly', 'run lightly'; 'walk cautiously', 'walk hurriedly', 'walk nervously').

Use the word 'adverb' when giving instructions.

As the children develop their understanding of movement to adverbs, introduce adverbs of degree (e.g. 'walk very quickly', 'walk extremely slowly').

Discuss with the children different ways in which they might move and different words that could be used to describe their movements. By referring to terms used in literacy lessons in lessons that involve physical activity, you will make the use of such terms more real for the children.

DEVELOPING STORY OPENERS

An activity that will help children appreciate the role adverbs and adverbial phrases can play in making text more interesting.

RESOURCES

Examples of texts that lack adverbs.

WHAT TO DO

In shared reading, look at a sentence that might be improved by introducing adverbs. For example:

Kate walked home.

Ask the children to suggest ways in which the sentence could be made more interesting and informative by adding adverbs. These might include:

Kate walked home slowly/sadly/hesitantly/nervously.

Discuss rearranging the sentence so that the adverb or adverbial phrase is placed at the beginning (a fronted adverbial):

Nervously, Kate walked home.

Filled with trepidation, Kate walked home.

Provide a selection of simple sentences and ask children to work together to develop them using adverbs and adverbial phrases. You might suggest that the sentence should be a story opener and that children should try to make it grab readers' attention and make them want to find out what happens next.

REFERENCE

DfE (2013) *The National Curriculum*. London: DfE.

FURTHER READING

Waugh, D., Warner, C. and Waugh, R. (2019) *Teaching Grammar, Punctuation and Spelling in Primary Schools* (3rd edition). London: SAGE, Chapter 2.

USEFUL WEBSITE

For information about some teaching implications for adverbs, see **www.cybergrammar.co.uk/ word_classes_adverbs_teach.php**

14

PRONOUNS

WHAT DO I NEED TO KNOW?

A pronoun can replace a noun, a noun phrase or another pronoun. We use pronouns such as 'he', 'her', 'it' and 'you' to make sentences less repetitive.

Look at this piece of writing and see how you might improve it by replacing 'Callum' in places:

> *Once upon a time there was a boy called Callum and Callum was not very clever. Callum lived in a house with his mum and dad and his sister. Callum's sister was always fighting him and Callum did not like her. Callum's dad is a lorry driver and he often drives his lorry to France. Sometimes Callum goes with him. I like Callum because he is good at football and he always shares his sweets with me.*

You might have decided to change the text to something like this:

> *Once upon a time there was a boy called Callum and <u>he</u> was not very clever. <u>He</u> lived in a house with his mum and dad and his sister. <u>His</u> sister was always fighting him and <u>he</u> did not like her. Callum's dad is a lorry driver and he often drives his lorry to France. Sometimes Callum goes with him. I like Callum because he is good at football and he always shares his sweets with me.*

You will probably have decided that it was not possible to replace every 'Callum' with a pronoun, because the text could become confusing if the reader was not sure which 'he' was being referred to, especially once Callum's father has been introduced. However, removing the constant repetition of the proper noun 'Callum' makes the text more readable and less repetitive.

Pronouns are essential to help us write concisely and without repetition. However, if we overuse pronouns, the reader can become confused and unsure whom the pronouns refer to.

There are both *subject* and *object* pronouns:

SUBJECT	OBJECT
I	me
he	him

she	her
we	us
they	them

So, in the sentence 'Callum lived in a house with his mum and dad and his sister', 'Callum' is the subject, and when we replace 'Callum' with a pronoun we use 'He'.

However, in the sentence 'I like Callum', 'Callum' is the object and 'I' is the subject, and when we replace 'Callum' with a pronoun we use 'him'.

WHAT IS IT USEFUL TO KNOW?

There are different kinds of pronouns.

PERSONAL PRONOUNS

Nearly all the pronouns we use in English are personal pronouns, used in place of a noun that refers to a specific person or people. Unlike the nouns, the structure changes according to their role in a sentence. They may be the subject of the sentence or clause:

James is my brother. <u>He</u> loves horses.

<u>We</u> went to the park together.

Our friends were there and <u>they</u> were playing.

Or they may be the direct or indirect object of the verb:

I passed the ball to <u>him</u>.

The bus driver didn't see <u>us</u>.

The teacher told <u>them</u> to go away.

POSSESSIVE PRONOUNS

Possessive pronouns, as the name suggests, are used to show ownership of something:

That book is <u>mine</u>.

My dad is bigger than <u>yours</u>.

The girls said the new house was bigger than <u>theirs</u>.

Possessive pronouns never use apostrophes, apart from those ending in one's (someone's, anyone's etc.). The only time 'its' has an apostrophe is when it is short for 'it is'.

REFLEXIVE PRONOUNS

Reflexive pronouns refer back to a person who has been mentioned previously:

He looked at <u>himself</u> in the mirror.

The girls soon learnt to care for <u>themselves</u>.

Have you hurt <u>yourself</u>?

These reflexive forms are also sometimes used for emphasis:

I don't see it <u>myself</u>.

The inspector said he would go <u>himself</u>.

Possessives are sometimes used incorrectly; it is not uncommon to see uses such as:

Please see Sue or myself for more information. *(this should correctly be 'Sue or me')*

Should we return the forms to yourself? *(this should correctly be 'to you')*

KEY KNOWLEDGE SUMMARY

WHAT ARE PRONOUNS?

Pronouns are words used in place of a noun that has recently been referred to, to save repetition.

WHAT ARE PERSONAL PRONOUNS?

These are the pronouns used when replacing a reference to a person. Personal pronouns are sometimes also used for emphasis.

IN THE CLASSROOM

Children should understand that pronouns only have capital letters when they begin sentences, with the exception of the personal pronoun 'I', which always has a capital, regardless of where it appears in a sentence:

I love football.

Jadon Sancho is better at football than I am.

In the English National Curriculum (DfE, 2013), children should, by the time they have completed Year 4, be able to make appropriate choices of pronoun or noun within and across sentences to aid cohesion and avoid repetition. By Year 5–6, they should be able to use relative pronouns to join clauses and implied (i.e. omitted) relative pronouns.

Relative pronouns such as 'who', 'which' or 'that' refer back to a noun, though the relative pronoun 'that' is often omitted. For example:

This is the dog that bit me last week. *(the sentence needs 'that' to make sense)*

It is the dog that I saw in the park.

It is the dog I saw in the park. *(the use of 'that' is unnecessary)*

When children are writing, they can overuse pronouns so that it gets confusing:

The pirates attacked the islanders, and they fought back bravely but they had more weapons, and they were not expecting them, so they found it easy to beat them …

It can be a useful exercise to get them to read their work back aloud, to make sure that the sense is not lost.

Another common mistake arises from the fact that in English, we have no non-gender-specific word for 'his or her'. This often leads people to use the plural form of the possessive, and say things such as:

Each child has brought their book.

The correct sentence would be:

Each child has brought his or her book.

This is fine once in a while, but it can look silly if used too frequently:

Each child sat on his or her chair, opened his or her book and began his or her work.

A better solution is to change the singular subject to a plural, if you can:

All the children sat on their chairs …

The use of they and their as singular pronouns is increasingly common and considered acceptable, especially in non-binary gender situations.

CLASSROOM ACTIVITIES

FIRST AND THIRD PERSON

An oral activity that encourages children to use different pronouns and to consider what happens to verbs in the third person.

RESOURCES

Lots of examples of stories and other texts. These might be extracts, or you could simply gather books together and put bookmarks into the pages you wish to read.

WHAT TO DO

Show the children some examples of text written in the first person and some written in the third person – ideally display one of each at the same time. Ask them to say what they notice about each. Talk about the first person and third person and explain that the second person ('you' and so on) is not often used in writing, except in instructional texts.

Ask the children which works best and which they prefer. What do we gain and lose when the first person is used? What do we gain and lose when the third person is used?

The third person of English verbs is usually different from the first and second person, with 's' added to most verbs – 'I like', 'you like', 'she likes' and so on.

Talk about this as you try writing sentences in different ways with the children. You can develop this as an oral activity by asking the children to take turns to say something about themselves. For example:

> *My name is Tom and I like ice cream.*

Then ask the child to point to someone else and say the same information about that person:

> *Your name is Sam and you like ice cream.*

Then ask Sam to tell the class about Tom:

> *His name is Tom and he likes ice cream.*

Talk about the different pronouns that are used and about the change to the verb in the third person.

Next, provide a set of sentences on individual cards and hand them out to the children. Ask them to change each from first to third person or from third to first person. This can be done orally but might be developed into a written activity. The children can go on to create their own sentences for each other, with an emphasis on making them interesting and, if appropriate for the children, multi-claused.

REFERENCE

DfE (2013) *The National Curriculum*. London: DfE.

USEFUL WEBSITES

For useful material and free downloads, see **www.bbc.co.uk/skillswise/topic/pronouns**

For a simple pronoun game, see **www.bbc.co.uk/skillswise/game/en27pron-game-personal-pronouns-treasure-hunt**

Try the travelling pronouns game available at **www.bbc.co.uk/bitesize/ks1/literacy/ pronouns/play/**

Try the pronoun game available at **www.softschools.com/language_arts/grammar/ pronoun/balloon_game/**

For more information about pronouns, see **http://oxforddictionaries.com/words/pronouns** and **www.grammarbook.com/grammar/pronoun.asp**

15

PREPOSITIONS

WHAT DO I NEED TO KNOW?

Prepositions are used to show the relationship between nouns or pronouns and other words in sentences. For example:

The pan was on the hob.

The preposition 'on' shows where the pan is in relation to the hob.

The cat hid behind the sofa.

The preposition 'behind' shows where the cat is in relation to the sofa.

Common prepositions include 'about', 'above', 'across', 'against', 'along', 'among', 'around', 'at', 'before', 'behind', 'below', 'beneath', 'beside', 'between', 'beyond', 'by', 'down', 'during', 'except', 'for', 'from', 'in', 'inside', 'into', 'like', 'near', 'of', 'off', 'on', 'since', 'through', 'to', 'toward', 'under', 'until' and 'up'.

One teacher told her pupils that 'a preposition is anywhere a mouse can go'. Look at the words above and see if this is true. Begin your sentence with 'The mouse ran …' and see if each of the prepositions could fit.

Prepositions usually precede nouns or pronouns – the word 'preposition' comes from the idea of being pre-positioned or positioned before. In the sentences below, the prepositions all precede nouns or pronouns. Can you identify them?

The cow jumped over the moon.

Coppinger kicked the ball into the goal.

Sara ran across the field.

If you decided that the prepositions were 'over', 'into' and 'across', you were correct. Sometimes, however, prepositions can be placed after nouns or pronouns. For example:

I gave up because I couldn't get through.

He took his coat off.

He left his dog behind.

Some people object to placing prepositions at the ends of sentences, but even if they were correct it is often impossible to avoid doing so without making sentences seem ridiculous. Look at the three sentences above and rearrange them so that the prepositions do not appear at the end of the sentences.

'He took off his coat' sounds fine.

'He left behind his dog' sounds awkward and confusing.

What would you do to avoid ending the first sentence with 'through'?

Winston Churchill, when criticised for ending a sentence with a preposition, is supposed to have replied, 'This is the kind of nonsense up with which I shall not put!' (see below for more examples).

WHAT IS IT USEFUL TO KNOW?

As you saw in the first section, most prepositions are single words such as 'up', 'down', 'over', 'on' or 'behind'. These are called simple prepositions. Where two or three words are used, we refer to complex prepositions. For example, two-word prepositions include 'ahead of', 'because of', 'along with' and 'except for'.

Three-word prepositions, also sometimes called complex or compound prepositions, include 'as well as', 'by means of' and 'in relation to'. These prepositional phrases often give a rather stuffy legal air to writing and are better avoided – there is nearly always a simpler and clearer alternative.

Prepositions often indicate time (e.g. 'at noon', 'during September', 'on Tuesday', 'since last year'), position (e.g. 'on the hill', 'up a tree') or direction (e.g. 'to Bolton', 'under the bridge'). They can also indicate possession (e.g. 'of his time'), means (e.g. 'by train') and accompaniment (e.g. 'with salt and vinegar').

It may be helpful to point out to children that the word preposition contains 'position' – this can help them to remember the term.

KEY KNOWLEDGE SUMMARY

WHAT IS A PREPOSITION?

Prepositions show the relationship between words in a sentence, usually with reference to place or time. They are usually single words but may be complex prepositions using two or more words. Prepositions usually refer to nouns.

IN THE CLASSROOM

Children need to develop an understanding of the use of the most common prepositions: 'about', 'above', 'across', 'against', 'along', 'among', 'around', 'at', 'before', 'behind', 'below', 'beneath', 'beside', 'between', 'beyond', 'by', 'down', 'during', 'except', 'for', 'from', 'in', 'inside', 'into', 'like', 'near', 'of', 'off', 'on', 'since', 'through', 'to', 'toward', 'under', 'until' and 'up'.

A useful strategy for doing this is to create some sentences in which the preposition could be changed so that the meaning of the sentence is changed. For example:

> *Sally ran along the road.*

Look at the prepositions above and see how many of them could replace 'along'. You could, for example, have:

> *Sally ran down the road.*
>
> *Sally ran near the road.*
>
> *Sally ran across the road.*
>
> *Sally ran up the road.*
>
> *Sally ran beside the road.*
>
> *Sally ran on the road.*

By discussing alternative prepositions with children, you will encourage them to be more precise in their writing, as well as helping them to vary their vocabulary.

It is incorrect to teach children that sentences cannot end with prepositions. This is a widespread idea, as mentioned earlier. Some sentences do sound ugly if they end with prepositions: for instance, it is fine to suggest changing 'The boy I gave the book to' to 'The boy to whom I gave the book', or 'This is the place I told you about' to 'This is the place about which I told you'. However, nowadays, such usages as the first of each pair are becoming more acceptable.

There are also many sentences in which it would be very long-winded even to try to avoid a preposition at the end. For instance, how could you rephrase these?

> *Hanif said he had left his coat behind.*
>
> *The nurse put the tablets on the top shelf and the blankets down below.*
>
> *She gazed at the sky above.*
>
> *She told him to put his pen down.*
>
> *He couldn't wait to look inside.*
>
> *He picked his boots up and put them on.*
>
> *If you cook the meal, I'll wash up.*

Or even:

What's a preposition for but to end a sentence with?

CLASSROOM ACTIVITIES

READING AND CREATING POEMS USING PREPOSITIONS

An activity that focuses attention on structure and pattern in language and which can be used to draw attention to the use of prepositions.

RESOURCES

Either use the poem below or create one of your own in which all, or virtually all, lines follow the same pattern.

ENERGY

Galloping through the playground

Running out of the gate

Rushing home from school

Dashing round the corner

Skipping along the road

Leaping over the hedge

Racing down the path

Hurrying through the door

Charging up the stairs

Bouncing on the bed

Jumping up and down

Bounding down the stairs

Gulping down some food

Falling fast asleep

(Jolliffe and Waugh, 2000)

WHAT TO DO

Read the poem to the children and discuss it. Then ask them to work in pairs to write an extra line to be inserted wherever they choose. Emphasise that it must follow the same pattern as the other lines (verb-preposition-determiner-noun). The last line is an exception, and you might ask the children why this might be so. They could even replace the last line with one that has the same pattern as the others.

Gather their ideas and write some of these on the board. Ask the children if the lines follow the correct pattern and invite them to suggest what the pattern is. Discuss the different word classes and focus on the prepositions. Ask the children to suggest some prepositions that are not found in the poem, and list these or create a prepositions chart that the children can refer to.

Now ask the children to work in pairs or independently to write their own poem in the same style as 'Energy'.

OTHER ACTIVITIES

For younger children, a cardboard box and a teddy bear can be used to get children to suggest prepositions to say where the teddy is (under, above, inside, behind and so on). This activity can also be used with older children in modern foreign languages lessons as they learn prepositions from another language.

For a storytelling or story-writing activity, introduce some possible story openings that begin with prepositions or prepositional phrases such as:

Throughout the day, rain had fallen …

During the night, there was an eerie screeching sound …

Deep in the woods, an owl hooted …

Ask the children to make their own suggestions and then use one to begin a piece of shared writing, modelling a narrative style and making use of prepositions. Then ask the children to write their own story openings in a similar style.

REFERENCE

Jolliffe, W. and Waugh, D. (2000) *Further Curriculum Bank Writing at Key Stage One*. Leamington Spa: Scholastic.

FURTHER READING

Waugh, D., Warner, C. and Waugh, R. (2019) *Teaching Grammar, Punctuation and Spelling in Primary Schools* (3rd edition). London: SAGE, Chapter 2.

16

DETERMINERS

WHAT DO I NEED TO KNOW?

A determiner is a word used to give more information about a noun by defining it as something specific or something of a particular type. The words that can fulfil this function may be *articles*, *demonstratives*, *possessive determiners* or *quantifiers*.

The definite article 'the' refers to a specific person, place or thing. For example:

The doctor who saved my life.

The dog I ran over last week.

The avenue I live in.

The indefinite articles 'a' and 'an' refer to any person, place or thing. 'An' is used before a word beginning with a vowel sound. For example:

A doctor can save your life.

A dog can be a good pet.

An avenue is a kind of street.

But note that some words which begin with 'u' have a consonant sound and so we tend to use 'a' with them. For example:

a useless watch

a uniform

a Ukrainian

'Some' is used as the plural form of the indefinite article. For example:

Some dogs are very noisy.

For lots of activities and ideas for teaching about determiners, see **https://sites.google.com/site/easygrammar4kids/a-an**

DEMONSTRATIVES

A demonstrative determiner is one which emphasises that a particular noun is being referred to (e.g. 'this evening', 'those trainers').

There are four demonstrative determiners in English: 'this', 'that', 'these' and 'those'.

Demonstrative determiners can also be used as demonstrative pronouns. When they are used as determiners, they are followed by the nouns they modify. Compare:

> This house is mine. *(demonstrative used as a determiner modifying the noun 'house')*

> This is my house. *(demonstrative used as a pronoun)*

POSSESSIVES

Possessive determiners, or possessive adjectives, refer to nouns by telling who they belong to. They are different from possessive pronouns – 'mine', 'his', 'hers', 'yours', 'ours' and 'their'.

The possessive adjectives are 'my', 'your', 'his', 'her', 'its', 'our', 'your' and 'their'.

Possessive pronouns can stand alone and are not followed by nouns.

Possessive determiners are followed by nouns.

Look at the examples below:

> This is <u>my</u> friend. *('my' is a possessive determiner, qualifying the noun 'friend')*

> My shoes are older than <u>yours</u>. *('yours' is a possessive pronoun, not followed by a noun)*

QUANTIFIERS

Quantifiers are followed by nouns that they qualify. Examples of quantifiers include: 'some', 'any', 'few', 'little', 'more', 'much', 'many', 'each', 'every', 'both', 'all', 'enough', 'half', 'little', 'whole', 'less', and both ordinal and cardinal numbers.

Quantifiers are commonly used before either count or non-count nouns. For example:

> He eats <u>more</u> pies than his friend.

> <u>Little</u> rain has fallen this month.

> <u>Forty</u> soldiers entered at once.

For more information on determiners, see **www.myenglishpages.com/site_php_files/grammar-lesson-determiners.php**

WHAT IS IT USEFUL TO KNOW?

'A' AND 'AN' BEFORE 'H'

Some English words start with an unpronounced 'aitch' ('h'). We use 'an' instead of 'a' for these (e.g. 'an hour', 'an honest person', 'an honour'), but not words where the 'h' is pronounced.

In spoken English, it is not uncommon to hear reference to 'an historic occasion', as it is easier to give stress to the word this way, although we tend to say 'a history lesson'. Most people would probably say 'a hotel', but some may refer to 'an hotel'.

PRONOUNCING 'THE'

'The' is the most common word in the English language and yet it can be pronounced in different ways.

'The' is pronounced (but not spelled) 'thee' for emphasis and before words that begin with vowels. Try saying each of the following:

the deer	the antelope
the chair	the armchair

We also pronounce 'the' as 'thee' when we want to emphasise something:

Are you the man who won those medals at the Olympics?

Are you the ('thee') Mo Farah or just someone with the same name as the great athlete?

ZERO DETERMINERS

There are many contexts where determiners are not used in English:

- with proper nouns (e.g. 'Emily Bronte', 'Belgium', 'Orion');

- with generalisations (e.g. 'cats are independent', 'laughter is good for you'); and

- when referring to an unspecified amount or number (e.g. 'he saw sparrows on the fence').

This kind of usage is sometimes referred to as 'zero determiner'.

USES OF DETERMINERS

A determiner can be a cohesive device, as it can refer back to an earlier noun. For example, we might say:

A large brown dog rummaged in a dustbin. The dog was very hungry.

KEY KNOWLEDGE SUMMARY

Demonstratives are words that define a noun in a sentence. Determiners may be articles (definite or indefinite), quantifiers (defining how much – all numbers are quantifiers), possessive (defining who something belongs to) or demonstrative (identifying a specific item). Try identifying the determiners in these examples:

Your dog is a nuisance.

I want some chocolate.

This exercise is easy.

My friend lives in Bradford.

The class completed three exercises.

His car broke down.

That car is always breaking down.

Her phone is a Samsung.

Some cars break down all the time.

I don't like those shoes.

IN THE CLASSROOM

Children sometimes use 'them' as a determiner because it can be used in some contexts similar to 'those', such as:

I saw those.

I saw them.

'Them' is a pronoun, however, and cannot be used as a determiner in Standard English. Such usages as 'them ones' are not Standard English but may feature in some dialects. Look at the sentences below and see how you would correct them:

I want them books tidied up.

Them boys shouldn't have thrown stones.

Try creating sentences with missing determiners and ask children to suggest which determiners could fill the spaces. For example:

Joe saw ___ great game.

Charis enjoyed ___ play.

___ people don't like chocolate but ___ people do.

I don't have ___ money.

Notice how there is often more than one possible missing word.

Some languages do not use articles such as 'the' and 'a', and this is something that may cause problems for non-native speakers.

ORIGINS OF ENGLISH DETERMINERS

The and that are common developments from the same Old English system. Old English had a definite article se, in the masculine gender, seo (feminine), and þæt (neuter). In Middle English these had all merged into þe, the ancestor of the Modern English word the.

(http://en.wikipedia.org/wiki/English_articles)

YE OLDE TEA SHOPPE

Have you ever wondered why some businesses use 'ye' instead of 'the' in their names? Think of 'Ye Olde White Hart' and 'Ye Olde Copper Kettle'. Wikipedia provides an explanation:

In Middle English, the (þe) was frequently abbreviated as a þ with a small e above it, similar to the abbreviation for that, which was a þ with a small t above it. During the latter Middle English and Early Modern English periods, the letter thorn (þ) in its common script, or cursive, form came to resemble a y shape. As such the use of a y with an e above it as an abbreviation became common. This can still be seen in reprints of the 1611 edition of the King James Version of the Bible in places such as Romans 15:29, or in the Mayflower Compact. Historically the article was never pronounced with a y sound, even when so written, although the modern, pseudo-archaic usage such as Ye Olde Englishe Tea Shoppe can be pronounced with a y sound.

(http://en.wikipedia.org/wiki/English_articles)

CLASSROOM ACTIVITIES

CHANGING DETERMINERS

This activity encourages discussion about sentence structure and the roles of words within sentences.

RESOURCES

You will need a set of sentences that include singular noun phrases. For example:

A large fierce tiger roared as it emerged from the jungle.

The small car was parked by the river.

WHAT TO DO

Look at one of the sentences with your class and read it aloud. Then change a determiner in a noun phrase. For example:

Some large fierce tiger roared as it emerged from the jungle.

Read the sentence again with the children and ask them what is wrong with it. What needs to change now that 'a' has been changed to 'some'?

Help them to identify amendments so that the sentence becomes, for example:

Some large fierce tigers roared as they emerged from the jungle.

Talk about the reasons for the changes. For example, once 'some' has replaced 'a', the tiger needs to become plural and the pronoun 'it' also needs to be plural.

Continue the activity with other sentences before providing some examples for the children to discuss and change in pairs. Go on to ask them to produce sentences for each other to change.

17

CONJUNCTIONS

WHAT DO I NEED TO KNOW?

Conjunctions, or connectives, are the words that join or connect words within a sentence, or parts of sentences. The commonest conjunctions are 'and' and 'but'; other common examples would include 'because', 'although', 'until' and 'or'.

Coordinating conjunctions join items that are of equal importance in a sentence:

> *You can have a hot dog <u>or</u> a burger.*
>
> *My brother waved his arm <u>and</u> shouted.*
>
> *The rain stopped <u>but</u> the wind was still blowing.*

Subordinating conjunctions connect subordinate clauses to the main clause of a sentence:

> *I carried on working <u>until</u> the bell rang.*
>
> *The old man fell asleep <u>because</u> he was exhausted.*

STARTING A SENTENCE WITH A CONJUNCTION

Many people have been taught that it is wrong to start a sentence with a conjunction. However, this is not so. It is not grammatically incorrect and is often the best way to make a dramatic point. For instance:

> *And furthermore, he returned the very same night!*
>
> *But this was by no means the last time they would see the mysterious stranger.*
>
> *Because you have been very good, you may have five minutes' extra playtime.*

FORM

Conjunctions have three basic forms:

1. single word (e.g. 'and', 'or', 'but', 'because', 'although');

2.   compound, often ending with 'as' or 'that' (e.g. 'so that', 'provided that', 'as long as', 'in order that'); and

3.   correlative, in two parts, surrounding an adverb or adjective (e.g. 'so … that').

POSITION

Coordinating conjunctions always come between the words or clauses that they join:

> I like cheese <u>but</u> I don't like onions.
>
> The dog was enormous <u>and</u> friendly.

Subordinating conjunctions usually come at the beginning of the subordinate clause:

> The boys stayed in <u>because</u> it was raining. Or <u>Because</u> it was raining, the boys stayed in.
>
> We waited <u>until</u> everyone had left.

WHAT IS IT USEFUL TO KNOW?

CONNECTIVES AND CONJUNCTIONS

The term 'connective' is often used interchangeably with the term 'conjunction'. Conjunctions are connectives, but some sources maintain that connectives can include phrases such as 'despite that' and 'in other words', while conjunctions are single words such as 'and' and 'but'. Other sources state that the two terms have identical meanings and that the term 'connective' is used because it makes it clearer what the function of such words is.

Some sources distinguish between conjunctions and connectives, stating that connectives are words or phrases that link clauses or sentences, whereas conjunctions link ideas *within* a sentence. It is argued by these sources that connectives can be conjunctions (e.g. 'but', 'when', 'because') or connecting adverbs (e.g. 'however', 'then', 'therefore'), but that there is a separate category of connectives which link clauses and sentences (e.g. 'firstly', 'secondly', 'thirdly', 'finally', 'eventually', 'then', 'next', 'later', 'above all', 'in particular', 'especially', 'significantly', 'indeed', 'notably', 'therefore', 'however', 'also', 'as well as', 'moreover', 'furthermore', 'consequently', 'in conclusion', 'nevertheless', 'on the other hand', 'meanwhile', 'afterwards', 'alternatively', 'otherwise', 'for example', 'in addition').

The *Oxford Dictionary Online* states:

> A conjunction (also called a connective) is a word such as and, because, but, for, if, or, and when. Conjunctions are used to connect phrases, clauses, and sentences.

(www.oxforddictionaries.com/words/conjunctions)

Interestingly, the National Curriculum in England only uses the term 'conjunction', while the National Literacy Strategy uses both terms, as does the Primary Literacy Framework.

There does not appear to be a definitive answer. For an interesting discussion among teachers about conjunctions and connectives, see **http://community.tes.co.uk/tes_primary/f/36/t/189249.aspx**

KEY KNOWLEDGE SUMMARY

There is no clearly agreed distinction between the terms 'connectives' and 'conjunctions' – both terms refer to words that link words in a sentence or link two parts of a sentence together. However, the National Curriculum does not use the term 'connective'. Coordinating conjunctions link two ideas of equal importance, while subordinating conjunctions emphasise one part over another. Most conjunctions are single words; there are a very few short phrases, called compound conjunctions.

IN THE CLASSROOM

The English National Curriculum (DfE, 2013) only mentions conjunctions in Year 3–4 and in the glossary. In their writing, Year 3–4 children should develop their understanding by:

- extending the range of sentences with more than one clause by using a wider range of conjunctions, including 'when', 'if', 'because' and 'although'; and

- using conjunctions, adverbs and prepositions to express time and cause.

There is no mention of connectives in the English curriculum, and so no need to introduce the term.

What children need to know, regardless of which term is used, is that conjunctions/connectives can play an important role in drawing ideas together in their writing, as well as in separating them. They also need to understand that such words and phrases are useful when they need to relate things to each other and to show the passage of time in their writing.

MISCONCEPTIONS ABOUT CONJUNCTIONS

The old misconception about not starting a sentence with a conjunction is still very strong, and children often need to be told specifically that it is not wrong.

Perhaps the misunderstanding has arisen from helping children to avoid incomplete sentences. Of course, they should not be encouraged to write such structures as:

We had sausages, crisps, and cake. And ice cream.

This would need to be revised into a single sentence, with the comma and 'and' before cake removed.

We had sausages, crisps, cake, and ice cream.

Children often tend to answer questions that ask 'why' with an answer that starts with 'because', and may need to be shown that these are not complete sentences:

Why did the windmill's sails turn?

Because the wind was blowing. *(it's the answer, but it's not a whole sentence)*

The sails turned because the wind was blowing.

'Because the wind was blowing' is a subordinate clause, and cannot stand as a whole sentence, but we could write:

Because the wind was blowing, the sails turned.

USING COMMAS WITH CONJUNCTIONS

When just two words or phrases are joined by a conjunction, no comma is needed:

Dancers in leotards and tutus performed on the stage.

However, when two or more items are listed, those items should be separated by commas:

Dancers in leotards, tutus and feathered headdresses performed on the stage.

No comma is generally used between the last item but one and the conjunction:

Sara bought bananas, apples, pears, grapes and celery.

I love broccoli, carrots, beans and tomatoes.

However, it may be necessary to use a comma (often referred to as the 'Oxford comma') for the sake of clarity, as in the examples below.

In a list of paired items, commas are used to show the parings, and in these cases a comma before the last pair is needed for clarity:

The menu offered fish and chips, sausage and mash, curry and rice, and bacon and eggs.

The correct answers to the quiz were Batman and Robin, Jekyll and Hyde, Peter Pan and Wendy, and Jack and Jill.

Similarly, when two complete sentences or main clauses are joined by a conjunction, we generally place a comma before the conjunction:

The different seasons come and go, and the trees constantly change their foliage to delight us.

No comma is needed in the phrase 'come and go', but we place a comma before the second 'and', which joins the two main clauses.

CLASSROOM ACTIVITIES

JOINING SENTENCES

A simple activity in which sentences are combined. This approach has been shown to be one of the most effective ways of teaching grammar and is widely used in the US (see Andrews et al., 2006; Myhill et al., 2011).

RESOURCES

Create a series of short, simple sentences such as:

I like chocolate.

I enjoy going to the cinema.

My friend buys me presents.

I go to the shop.

You could write these on pieces of card or have them on a whiteboard or interactive whiteboard (IWB). The important thing is that you can move them around.

Make cards with a different conjunction on each one (e.g. 'and', 'but', 'because', 'therefore', 'when').

WHAT TO DO

Look at pairs of simple sentences with the children and ask them to suggest ways in which they might be joined to create a single, compound sentence using a conjunction. For example:

I like chocolate.

I go to the shop.

These could be joined as:

I go to the shop because I like chocolate.

You could go on to discuss ways in which other words and phrases might be added to the sentence to make it more meaningful. For example:

I go to the shop every day because I like to buy chocolate with my pocket money.

Look at other ways of connecting the sentences such as:

I go to the shop in order to buy chocolate because I like it.

DEVELOPMENT: COMMA SPLICES CORRECTED BY USING CONJUNCTIONS

The comma splice is a common error in written English. It involves connecting two clauses or sentences using a comma, which is usually insufficient for the job. Look at the sentences below and then choose a conjunction to replace the comma:

My dog is unhappy, he was stung by a wasp.

My car broke down, it is always doing that.

Gareth hates sausages, he doesn't like burgers either.

Can you see that the comma is insufficient to separate the clauses in these sentences? However, if we use conjunctions, we can improve them:

My dog is unhappy because he was stung by a wasp.

My car broke down and it is always doing that.

Gareth hates sausages and he doesn't like burgers either.

REFERENCES

Andrews, R., Torgerson, C., Beverton, S., Freeman, A., Locke, T., Low, G., Robinson, A. and Zhu, D. (2004) The effect of grammar teaching on writing development. *British Educational Research Journal*, 32(1): 39–55.

DfE (2013) *The National Curriculum*. London: DfE.

Myhill, D., Lines, H. and Watson, A. (2011) *Making Meaning with Grammar: A Repertoire of Possibilities*. University of Exeter, UK.

18

SYNONYMS AND ANTONYMS

WHAT DO I NEED TO KNOW?

Reading, writing, speaking and listening would be rather dull if there were only one word for each place, object or feeling. In English, we often have many ways of naming the same things. Synonyms and antonyms enrich our language and often originate from other languages.

WHAT ARE SYNONYMS?

Synonyms are words that have the same or very similar meaning. Nouns, verbs, adjectives, adverbs and prepositions can have a synonym as long as both words are the same part of speech.

EXAMPLES OF SYNONYMS

Adjectives: 'nice', 'pleasant', 'lovely'

Nouns: 'road', 'lane', 'street'

Verbs: 'love', 'adore', 'admire'

Prepositions: 'on', 'above', 'over'

Adverbs: 'quickly', 'swiftly', 'rapidly'

You could find many more examples, but the key point is that all of the above synonyms could be interchanged in a sentence. But when you replace a word with its synonym, you have to look at the context to ensure the synonym conveys the same meaning.

For example, you might tell someone, 'I love your new coat', but you almost certainly wouldn't tell someone, 'I worship your new coat'. And even though 'expire' and 'die' can be synonyms, you wouldn't say that your passport had died.

When people are using a language in which they are not fluent, they can often use inappropriate synonyms. Non-native speakers may say, for example, 'I have a big love of tennis', where a native speaker would say 'I have a great love of tennis'.

You can find a rich source of synonyms in a thesaurus.

WHAT ARE ANTONYMS?

Antonyms are words that have opposite meanings – antonym is the antonym of synonym! Some antonyms are created by putting a prefix (see Chapter 5) at the beginning of a word (e.g. 'happy'/'unhappy', 'like'/'dislike', 'possible'/'impossible'), while others involve using completely different words.

The antonym of 'good' is 'bad', but might also be 'evil', 'ill' and 'wicked', or even 'awful' and 'terrible'. As with synonyms, the context in which we use the words is important in determining the appropriate antonym. For example, the word 'light' could have the antonym 'dark' or 'heavy', depending upon context.

WHAT IS IT USEFUL TO KNOW?

TYPES OF ANTONYMS

We can divide antonyms into three categories: graded antonyms, complementary antonyms and relational antonyms.

GRADED ANTONYMS

Graded antonyms are word pairs rather like those you find in surveys where you are asked to rate something on a scale from very good to very poor. They refer to points on a spectrum.

Look at the examples below and decide which words might fit in between the extremes:

happy/sad

dark/light

dangerous/safe

wet/dry

COMPLEMENTARY ANTONYMS

Complementary antonyms are word pairs that have no degree of meaning. There are only two possibilities, either one or the other:

dead/alive

true/false

on/off

RELATIONAL ANTONYMS

Relational antonyms are pairs that have a direct relationship with each other:

husband/wife

predator/prey

parent/child

KEY KNOWLEDGE SUMMARY

Synonyms are words that have the same or very similar meaning (e.g. 'scared', 'frightened', 'terrified', 'petrified'). Antonyms are words that have opposite meanings, so 'antonym' is the antonym of 'synonym'. Some antonyms are created by putting a prefix at the beginning of a word (e.g. 'likely'/'unlikely', 'trust'/'distrust', 'behave'/'misbehave'), while others involve using completely different words (e.g. 'good'/'bad', 'tall'/'short').

IN THE CLASSROOM

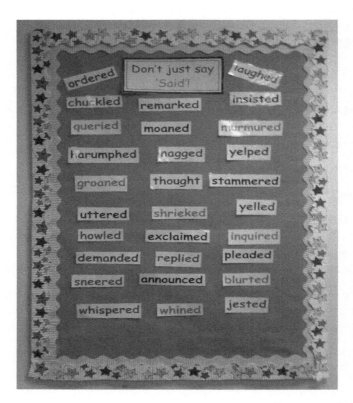

Figure 18.1   Don't just say 'said'.

Like many languages, English has many different words for similar items and emotions. Sometimes the same item has different names in different dialects or different regions.

Many children with English as an additional language (EAL) learn a basic vocabulary quite quickly and can soon converse. However, they may be confused when new words are used. It can be very helpful to create charts of different names for items and emotions. Children can do this using a thesaurus and through exploring some of the excellent websites that focus on dialects, including **www.bbc.co.uk/voices/schools/** and **https://sounds.bl.uk/Accents-and-dialects**

CLASSROOM ACTIVITIES

ANTONYM ACTIVITY: OPPOSITE ADVERBS – 'FORTUNATELY' AND 'UNFORTUNATELY'

This is a simple oral activity that can be developed into a written activity. It can be played by pairs of children, small groups or even the whole class. It focuses on adverb antonyms as fronted adverbials.

RESOURCES

Make a list of adverbial antonyms and have this available as a crib for the children. Prepare a sequence of sentences that begin alternately with 'fortunately' or 'unfortunately' and which tell a story or relate a series of events.

WHAT TO DO

Start off by modelling beginning sentences with 'fortunately' and 'unfortunately'. For example:

Fortunately, I'm going home early today.

Unfortunately, I have to go to the dentist.

Fortunately, nearly all of my teeth are in good condition.

Unfortunately, I have to have two taken out.

Now invite the children to try 'fortunately'/'unfortunately' sentences in pairs or threes – threes work well because the children have to make sentences for both 'fortunately' and 'unfortunately'.

Next, ask them to work in small groups, with each child writing a 'fortunately' sentence at the top of a piece of paper and then passing it to the person on his/her left to add an 'unfortunately' sentence. After a few minutes, invite the children to read aloud the paper they have in front of them.

Next time you use the activity, give different words for each group to work with (e.g. 'sadly'/'happily', 'foolishly'/'sensibly', 'silently'/'noisily', 'patiently'/'impatiently').

Discuss ways in which sentences with fronted adverbials are punctuated and encourage the children to look for examples in their reading.

COOPERATIVE WRITING USING PICTURES

This activity, which focuses on synonyms and can be adapted for all ages, is based upon a collection of stimulating pictures.

RESOURCES

Print or cut out from magazines a selection of pictures and then attach them to pieces of A3 paper with Blu-Tack.

WHAT TO DO

The activity has clear stages, but for younger or less confident children you may need to give a higher level of teacher modelling than for others. The possible stages are set out below, but some could be left out depending upon the children's abilities.

1. Mount two large pictures on the board and explain to the children that you have written a short description of one of them. Ask them to listen carefully as you read your description and to wait until you have finished before deciding which of the two pictures you are describing, supporting their judgement by referring to what you wrote. Display the description so that they can refer to it.

2. Leave the other large picture in the centre of the board (or use an interactive whiteboard with a picture in the centre, if available). Explain that you would like the children to help you to produce a description of the picture so that if it were displayed along with several others, anyone reading the description would be able to identify the picture. Ask the children to suggest short phrases to describe various features. For example, for a beach scene: 'clear, blue sky', 'white, sandy beach', 'crashing, white waves', 'bright, orange sun'. Write the children's suggestions in the space around the picture and continue to add to these as they have more ideas.

3. Having produced notes as the basis, ask the children to discuss how they might turn some of the phrases into sentences, finding synonyms for the first words, combining phrases or adding further adjectives and adverbs.

4. With the children's help, compose a short piece of descriptive writing to describe the picture. This could be prose, perhaps with a word limit of 50 words, or a poem with or without rhyme.

5. Provide each pair of children with a picture mounted on A3 paper and ask them to work together to make notes on the paper around the picture with descriptive phrases. These could include feelings generated by the picture, as well as descriptions of what can be seen.

6. After a few minutes, ask each pair to pass their picture and notes on to another pair, but not to discuss what they have written or to draw attention to errors. Ask the new pairs to look at what has already been written and then to add their own ideas.

7. Pass the pictures and notes on once more after a few minutes for further additions from another pair of children.

8.   Ask the children to return the pictures to their original writers and allow some discussion between all of the six authors involved.

9.   Explain that the original writers can now draw upon everyone's ideas to help them to produce a short descriptive piece of writing. Tell them that you will be displaying all of the pictures and all of the pieces of writing, but not next to each other. The writers need to make their descriptions good enough for readers to be able to match them to the appropriate pictures.

This activity features shared reading and writing, note-making, cooperative work, drafting, editing and revising, with many opportunities for word- and sentence-level study, as well as writing in different genres, and leads to accurate and careful presentation. You could try similar activities using artefacts – perhaps stones, leaves or pots – instead of pictures.

For examples of antonyms, see **http://examples.yourdictionary.com/examples-of-antonyms. html**

For activities related to antonyms, see **www.k12reader.com/synonyms-and-antonyms/**

FURTHER READING

Crystal, D (1987) *The Cambridge Encyclopedia of Language.* Cambridge: Cambridge University Press.

Waugh, D. (2013) 'Developing vocabulary', in D. Waugh and S. Neaum (eds), *Beyond Early Reading.* London: Critical Publishing.

19

SPELLING

WHAT DO WE NEED TO KNOW?

WHY DOES SPELLING MATTER?

Competent spellers do not need to spend time thinking about spelling, so they are free to think about compositional aspects of writing. Children who find spelling difficult often lack confidence in writing generally and write shorter, simpler pieces, avoiding adventurous vocabulary choices. Poor spelling may distract or even confuse the reader; some children's spelling is so weak that adults and even the children themselves may not be able to read back what they have written. Too many children, and indeed adults, label themselves as poor spellers rather than believing they can improve their spelling. It is important that children are taught spelling early, systematically and effectively to avoid this.

WHEN DOES SPELLING MATTER?

Spelling matters in finished writing that is to be presented to others. It is not so important in notes, first drafts and so on, particularly when these are for the writer's use only.

WHAT IS INVOLVED IN SPELLING?

In order to spell words, we need knowledge of the alphabetic system – the correspondence between graphemes (letters or groups of letters) and phonemes (the sounds of the spoken language). However, this knowledge is not enough, as there are often several plausible ways of representing a phoneme. Consider, for example, how the vowel sound is represented in the following words: 'saw', 'born', 'fought', 'caught', 'haunt' and 'mournful'.

The writer needs to know which of the possible spellings is the correct one for the chosen word. Although English spelling is less regular than that of many other languages, it does have some consistent rules and a large number of recognisable patterns. Mature spellers know the spellings of most of the words they use in their writing.

WHAT STRATEGIES DO GOOD SPELLERS USE?

Good spellers use a range of strategies to decide how to spell a word they are not sure of. They may use:

- a phonic approach (spelling it the way it sounds);

- analogy – spelling it like other known words (e.g. 'mission' and 'fission');

- knowledge of root words (e.g. 'finite', 'definite', 'infinite'); and

- a visual approach (e.g. writing the word in two or three different ways and deciding which looks right).

COMMON DIFFICULTIES IN SPELLING

Writers often have difficulties in the following areas:

- adding prefixes and suffixes to words;

- vowel choices in unstressed syllables (e.g. the second syllable in 'farmer', 'doctor');

- consonant doubling (e.g. 'embarrass' but 'harass'); and

- homophones – words that sound the same but are spelled differently (e.g. 'right' and 'rite').

For lists of common spelling errors, see **https://global.oup.com/booksites/content/0199296251/ essentials/commonspellingerrors/** and **https://www.lexico.com/en/grammar/common-misspellings**

WHAT IS IT USEFUL TO KNOW?

WHERE DO ENGLISH SPELLINGS COME FROM?

English spelling is more complex than many other languages because of the history of the language. The English language was brought to the country by the Angles, who arrived here in the first half of the fifth century AD. A high proportion of our words come from their Germanic language, including 'house', 'children', 'wood', 'island', 'wall' and 'name'. Other languages also added words to English, including:

- Old Norse (brought by the Vikings). Words such as 'egg', 'sky' and 'kneel' come from this source.

- Romance languages (Latin, French). These were the languages of the ruling class, of government and the Church. Words such as 'company', 'dance', 'hazard' and 'sacrifice' come from these languages.

- Greek – the language of areas of knowledge such as philosophy and maths (e.g. 'hypotenuse', 'physics', 'bishop' and 'telescope').

- Other languages (e.g. 'shampoo', 'veranda' and 'thug' are derived from Hindi).

New words are added to the language all the time, and these are not only loan words from other languages, but also newly invented words, often in response to technological developments. In each case, a decision is made about how the word will be spelled (e.g. 'byte' rather than 'bite' or 'bight', both of which already existed as words).

WHEN DID SPELLING BECOME STANDARDISED?

Spellings were not standardised until relatively late in the history of the language. The introduction of the printing press in the fifteenth century was a factor in this standardisation, but even a century later people did not even spell their own names consistently: on the six wills and other legal documents signed by Shakespeare he wrote his surname 'Shakper', 'Shakspear', 'Shakspea', 'Shackspere', 'Shakspere' and 'Shakspear'.

However, spellings were increasingly standardised, with decisions on the form adopted being taken for a variety of reasons: French scribes altered the Old English 'cw' in 'queen' to 'qu', while Flemish printers introduced the 'gh' they were familiar with from their own language to 'ghost'.

Dictionaries began as attempts to describe the language, but were increasingly seen as prescribing spellings. The *Oxford English Dictionary* (2000) describes itself as 'the definitive record of the English language'.

There are relatively few words where alternative spellings are permitted (e.g. 'jewelry' or 'jewellery' and 'judgment' or 'judgement').

AMERICAN SPELLING

Some words are spelled differently in the US, often using a simplified version (e.g. 'behavior', 'color' and 'honor'). American spellings use an '-ize' ending in words such as 'realize', where British spelling uses '-ise', and the British spellings 'practice' (noun) and 'practise' (verb) are reversed in American spelling.

KEY KNOWLEDGE SUMMARY

Spelling matters because it supports effective communication; being a good speller frees the writer up to think about other aspects of writing. Writers use a range of strategies to help them decide how to spell words.

IN THE CLASSROOM

ARE SOME CHILDREN NATURAL SPELLERS?

At one time, it was thought that children would learn spellings as they read, and that spelling did not need to be taught. Peters (1985) found that while this applied to a small minority of children, the majority did not absorb spellings in this way and needed to be taught. Children who find it difficult to remember spellings need early and systematic teaching so that they do not start to see themselves as bad spellers.

Children who find spelling easy tend to have:

- good language skills;

- good language support at home (families who are interested in words, in language and in language play);

- good visual discrimination (e.g. in 'spot the difference' activities);

- clear articulation (saying words clearly); and

- fast, flowing handwriting.

MARKING

It is important to gear assessment to purpose. Spelling is not important in notes or first drafts and should not be commented on. It is helpful if children are encouraged to cross out, not rub out, as their attempts to spell a word are often useful evidence of their knowledge and understanding and misconceptions they may have. It is also important to consider what learning may result from marking of spelling errors. How many spelling mistakes should be identified? Are the mistakes identified words that are often used, or words that the child has been taught? How is the child expected to respond?

GIVING SPELLINGS

When children copy spellings letter by letter, they are not learning to spell the words. If children are being given spellings, then rather than saying the sounds or letter names ('That's P-E-O-P-L-E, James') or writing the word for the child to copy, it is best to ask the child to write the word first. Then write it for them. Are the two versions the same? If not, what is different? What is the tricky bit of the word? What would have to be changed to make their version the same as the adult's? Finally, remove both versions, delay a few moments and then ask the child to write the word from memory. This process is much more likely to help the child remember how the word is spelled in the future.

CLASSROOM ACTIVITIES

INVESTIGATIONS

RESOURCES

You may need prepared word lists.

WHAT TO DO

Give the children a set of 20–30 words such as:

- words that only need '-s' to make them plural and those that need '-es';

- hard 'c' and soft 'c' words; and

- words that do and don't double the consonant when '-ing' is added.

Ask the children to look for patterns and generate a rule. Display the rule and continue to add examples over time. Can the children find any examples that break the rule?

BEST BET

This is an investigation of the most likely spelling pattern for a long vowel phoneme in a single syllable word (e.g. to investigate the long 'a').

RESOURCES

You may need prepared word lists.

WHAT TO DO

To investigate the long /ai/ phoneme, divide the children into nine groups and ask each group to write down all the words they can think of that rhyme with their given word ('cake', 'made', 'wage', 'base', 'pale', 'same', 'rain', 'cape', 'wait'). If this is likely to be difficult, provide sets of words for them. Ask the children to sort the words by spelling pattern and report back to the class. Which is the best bet when writing words with the different word endings? Which is the best bet for this vowel phoneme generally?

REFERENCES

Oxford University Press (2000) *Oxford English Dictionary* (2nd edition). Oxford: Oxford University Press.

Peters, M. (1985) *Spelling: Caught or Taught?* London: Routledge.

FURTHER READING

Crystal, D. (2005) *The Stories of English*. London: Penguin.

Crystal, D. (2012) *Spell It Out: The Singular Story of English Spelling*. London: Profile Books.

Jolliffe, W., Waugh, D. and Gill, A. (2019) *Teaching Systematic Synthetic Phonics in Primary Schools* (3rd edition). London: SAGE, Chapter 6.

O'Sullivan, O. and Thomas, A. (2007) *Understanding Spelling*. London: Routledge.

Waugh, D. and Jolliffe, W. (2017) *English 5–11: A Guide for Teachers* (3rd edition). London: Routledge, Chapter 12.

Waugh, D., Warner, C. and Waugh, R. (2019) *Teaching Grammar, Punctuation and Spelling in Primary Schools* (3rd edition). London: SAGE.

20

HOW TO LEARN A SPELLING

WHAT DO I NEED TO KNOW?

WHAT IS INVOLVED IN LEARNING A SPELLING?

To learn a spelling, we need to store the correct sequence of letters in our memory. If we were to do this with each word as an individual item, it would be a huge task; instead, we can often learn groups of words that share the same spelling pattern (e.g. 'could', 'would', 'should', 'mould', 'boulder'). We can also use our knowledge of the spelling system, whether implicit or explicit. We may know that English words do not end with the letter 'v', or we may simply feel that 'hav' and 'giv' do not look right. A spelling cannot be considered learned if the learner only remembers it long enough to pass a test; spellings, once learned, should be able to be produced at any time, and preferably written fast and without hesitation. This frees up the writer to concentrate on other aspects of writing.

In order to learn a spelling, we need to pay careful attention to the structure of the word. Often only a part of the word causes problems for the speller; in 'friend', for example, it is the 'ie' digraph and in 'because' the 'au' that typically causes difficulties for children, producing misspellings such as 'becase' and 'becuase'. It is important that children are encouraged to think about which part of the word is tricky for them, and focus on it when learning the spelling.

STRATEGIES FOR LEARNING SPELLINGS

- *Look/cover/write/check (or look/say/cover/write/check)*. This routine involves looking carefully at the structure of the word while saying it clearly. Then it is covered, written from memory and checked. The procedure is repeated to reinforce learning. It may help to say the letter names while writing.

- *Spelling rules*. These may be discovered through investigation and then applied to new words (e.g. rules for pluralising words ending in '-y').

- *Over-articulation of the word*. For words such as 'February' and 'library', it can help to say the word in an exaggerated way.

- *Mnemonics (pronounced 'nemonics')*. These are individual ways of remembering words that cause the writer particular problems, such as 'FRIday is the END of the week' for 'friend', or 'a PIEce of pie' for piece, or 'oh you lucky duck' for the '-ould' group of words.

WHICH WORDS SHOULD BE LEARNED?

Prioritise words that are likely to be used, as learning that is not applied is likely to be forgotten over time – and particularly high-frequency words regularly misspelled by the writer. This will significantly reduce the number of mistakes produced and will counter the 'overlearning' of the incorrect spelling. In other words, if we regularly write 'definate', that will look right to us because that is the version we are used to seeing.

Words learned by children are likely to include:

- their own 'problem' words;

- words using spelling patterns or rules that the class is investigating together;

- words related to topics, which are likely to be used often while the topic is being studied; and

- words from the lists in the National Curriculum programme of study.

WHAT IS IT USEFUL TO KNOW?

DEVELOPING AN INTEREST IN WORDS

Children who have an interest in words are likely to find it easier to learn spellings. Here are two examples of such children:

Lucy (4 years 10 months) asked spontaneously, 'Why is there an "e" in Nokes?'

Natalie, aged 5 years 6 months, was playing hangman with her father. She challenged him with a three-letter word. He ran confidently through all the vowel letters, including 'y', but she said no to each. Her father was baffled. The word turned out to be 'Mrs'.

This interest in words often comes from parents who themselves have an interest in language and talk about words with their children. Teachers can also develop children's interest in words – both their meanings and also why they are spelled as they are, as well as what exceptions do not conform to a pattern.

DEVELOPING THE VISUAL MEMORY

Children with good visual discrimination and a good visual memory are at an advantage when it comes to spelling. It is possible to improve both by practice. 'Spot the difference' or 'spot the similarity' activities develop visual discrimination, and these can work for words as well as pictures, as in these examples:

What is the same in 'wearing' and 'early'?

What is different in 'towel' and 'trowel'?

What smaller words can be found in 'father' (keeping the letters in the same order)?

The visual memory can be developed; when using look/cover/write/check to learn a spelling, it is important that children try to delay a little before writing the word, trying to 'see' the word in their heads before committing it to paper.

CONFIDENCE AND MOTIVATION

As with the learning of any skill, motivation is very important; children who want to learn to spell are more likely to be successful than those who do not. It is important that children believe they can improve their spelling if they work at it. If spelling sessions are short, well-paced and fun, with a variety of activities, children are more likely to enjoy learning to spell.

For example, see this song about commonly misspelled words: **www.youtube.com/ watch?v=I93ySM-PNKM**

KEY KNOWLEDGE SUMMARY

Spelling is a skill that depends on knowledge of the spelling system and an ability to judge whether words 'look right'. Children need to be able to select from a range of strategies for learning spellings.

IN THE CLASSROOM

TEACHING SPELLING: PRINCIPLES

- Spelling is a skill best taught and practised in regular short bursts.

- Teaching should focus on both spelling patterns and rules, as well as on learning and practising strategies for attempting unknown words and for learning spellings.

- If children are given spellings while they are writing, these should be words they need to learn, and there should be a focus on what is difficult about the word. Children should see the word and then write it from memory, not copy letter by letter.

GROUPING WORDS FOR LEARNING

It is important that words are grouped to reinforce the pattern to be learned. For example, 'whent' is a common misspelling. What group of words could be taught to tackle this mistake?

rent, dent, sent, lent, tent
web, well, wet, west, wedding
when, where, why, which, who

It is often thought that teaching 'sent', 'rent' and so on would be appropriate. However, the children who write 'whent' have no difficulty with the end of the word; their problem is the beginning, and the false analogy they have made with words such as 'where' and 'when'. 'Went' should therefore be taught with words such as 'web', 'wet' and 'west'.

SPELLING LISTS AND CLASS TESTS: ISSUES

Spelling lists may include words children do not know and will not use, or words they already know how to spell. Class spelling tests may not challenge children whose spelling is already very good, and may repeatedly seem to confirm to other children that they are 'no good' at spelling. Spellings that are right in the test may then be spelled wrongly in independent writing.

LEARNING SPELLINGS AT HOME

Parents may not be sure how to support their children. If spellings are sent home, clear guidance needs to be given. Sending spellings home is no substitute for regular, systematic and effective teaching of spelling at school.

SPELLING LOGS AND JOURNALS

These give independence in children's spelling learning and allow them to take responsibility for their own progress. Children can:

- list problem words they have identified from their own writing and practise them;

- record strategies they have used; and

- test each other on personal spelling lists.

SPELLING AND HANDWRITING

Peters (1985) and Cripps (1989) suggested that spelling and handwriting were closely linked. They argued that if children wrote in a cursive (joined) script, the flowing movement supported the learning of the correct sequence of letters in the word. Spellings can be practised not only by writing on paper or an individual whiteboard, but also by finger-tracing in the air, in a sand tray or on any convenient surface.

DICTIONARIES IN THE CLASSROOM

While children should not be looking up spellings while they write, it is appropriate for them to check words they were not sure of as part of the editing process. Dictionaries should be freely available for this purpose, and children need to learn dictionary skills: the quartiles (EMS) so that they start looking in the right part of the dictionary, and alphabetical order – to the second, third and fourth letters and so on – over time.

Types of dictionaries:

- *School dictionaries.* It is important that children have access to dictionaries that are likely to contain most if not all of the words they are likely to write.

- *Etymological dictionaries.* These give information about the origin of words as well as meaning, and are useful and interesting for older children.

- *The ACE Spelling Dictionary.* Useful for older children with spelling difficulties. It allows them to find a word whether they have any idea how to spell it or not (Moseley, 1995).

CLASSROOM ACTIVITIES

CHOOSING SPELLING STRATEGIES

RESOURCES

List of spellings drawn either from errors in the children's work, or from the National Curriculum lists, and interactive whiteboard/whiteboard/flip chart.

WHAT TO DO

Ask the children what strategies they use when learning spellings, and list them on the board. Remind the children of any strategies they have forgotten.

Give the children the first word to be learned and ask them in pairs to discuss the best strategy for learning the word. Do they agree? Ask the children to try out their selected strategy, and then report back. Repeat for other words. Discuss: Are some strategies best for particular words? Do some learners have favourite strategies? Why is it useful to have different ways of learning spellings?

THE MISSING LETTER GAME

RESOURCES

List of target words to learn, interactive whiteboard/whiteboard/flip chart, and individual whiteboards and pens.

WHAT TO DO

Write a target word on the board and discuss any tricky bits. Erase the word, and then model writing it, replacing one letter with an underscore each time, starting with the first and working through to the last. For example, for the word 'people', write:

_eople

p_ople

pe_ple

peo_le

peop_e

*peopl_*

Ask the children to do the same on their own boards. Repeat with other target words.

This activity is harder than might be expected, even with a known spelling, and is a very good way of focusing on the letters in sequence and storing the sequence in the memory.

REFERENCES

Cripps, C. (1989) *Joining the ABC*. Wisbech: LDA.

DfE (2013) *The National Curriculum*. London: DfE.

Moseley, D. (1995) *ACE Spelling Dictionary*. Wisbech: LDA.

Peters, M. (1985) *Spelling: Caught or Taught?* London: Routledge.

FURTHER READING

DCSF (2009) *Support for Spelling*. London: DCSF.

Mudd, N. (1994) *Effective Spelling*. London: Hodder & Stoughton.

O'Sullivan, O. and Thomas, A. (2007) *Understanding Spelling*. London: Routledge.

Waugh, D., Warner, C. and Waugh, R. (2019) *Teaching Grammar, Punctuation and Spelling in Primary Schools* (3rd edition). London: SAGE.

21

PHONICS AND SPELLING

WHAT DO YOU NEED TO KNOW?

In the early stages of writing development, children begin to understand that marks on paper represent sounds in the words they hear and use. This is because English has an alphabetic writing system; not all writing systems work in this way, but it is on the whole a highly efficient way of recording language.

In order to be able to write independently, children need to:

- hear the separate phonemes, or sounds, in words (e.g. the four phonemes in 'frog' – /f/ /r/ /o/ /g/) in sequence – this skill is called segmenting; and

- match a written symbol, or grapheme, to each phoneme.

English speakers use roughly 42 phonemes; the exact number depends on the speaker's accent. A child who knows one way of representing each phoneme in their spoken language can write anything, and much of the time their writing can be read, as the reader simply reverses the process the writer has gone through, sounding out each grapheme and then blending the phonemes to produce a word.

Learning to write would be a very straightforward process if each phoneme was represented by only one grapheme, and preferably a single-letter grapheme. Unfortunately, an alphabet of 26 letters cannot do this, so many sounds are represented by digraphs (two letters) such as 'oa' or 'ph', trigraphs (three letters) such as 'ore' or 'tch', or even more. And this is not the only complication.

In English, almost every phoneme can be represented in more than one way. Look at the following examples:

/or/ – 'fork', 'four', 'haul', 'saw', 'ball', 'taught', 'fought'

/s/ – 'sit', 'cell', 'fuss', 'science', 'psychic'

Thus, as children learn more about the alphabetic code, they discover they have choices as to how to represent each phoneme, and little to guide them in those choices. 'Wait' or 'wate'? 'Giant' or 'jiant'? Phonics does not provide an answer.

WHAT IS IT USEFUL TO KNOW?

PHONICS AND PHONOLOGY

Consider the following spelling errors from a child in Year 1:

TARGET WORD	CHILD'S ATTEMPT
drive	jriv
tree	chree
too	toow
very	vereey

At first sight, these may seem very odd attempts, but try saying the words aloud, slowly, and they make much more sense. The sound we use at the beginning of 'drive' is not the same as the one heard at the beginning of 'dog', and the sound at the beginning of 'tree' and 'train' is much more like the one at the beginning of 'chop' than the beginning of 'top'. Similarly, anyone who has ever watched a young writer painstakingly sounding out words such as 'too' and 'very' will know that as they 'stretch' the word, they do in fact hear all the sounds they then represent.

Try saying 'give it to anyone' and think about how you said 'to'. It probably sounded very much like the 'toow' in the table above, and different from the way it sounds in the phrase 'to me'. Sounds in words are affected by the sounds that come before and after them, and for initial and final sounds, the words that come before or after them.

The alphabetic code therefore can be seen not as an exact and unchanging matching of grapheme to phoneme, or written symbol to speech sound, but a fairly rough-and-ready matching, which has to allow for variations of accent as well as the issues explained above.

PHONICS IN LATER SPELLING DEVELOPMENT

Although phonic knowledge and phonological awareness do not provide children with everything they need in order to become good spellers, they do continue to underpin spelling development, even as a visual approach becomes more important.

Phonics helps children to write longer words, sounding them out syllable by syllable in order. It also allows children to read back what they have written to see that they have produced at the very least a plausible phonic representation of the target word. Children whose understanding of phonics is very weak may produce attempts at words that are nothing like the intended word, and which cannot be read by them or anyone else. It is good practice, when attempting an unknown word, to check back to ensure that it is a possible spelling (e.g. the name 'Deirdre' is often misspelled as 'Deidre', but the 'ei' grapheme cannot represent the /ear/ phoneme).

KEY KNOWLEDGE SUMMARY

Young writers use their phonic skills and knowledge to segment spoken words into individual phonemes or sounds, and then match written symbols (graphemes) to each sound. Graphemes can consist of one, two or more letters.

IN THE CLASSROOM
TEACHING PHONICS FOR WRITING

Segmenting is an essential skill, but some children find it difficult to 'hear' the individual phonemes in words. The skill is developed through oral activities, with extensive teacher modelling. It is important that there is not an overemphasis on the first sound in words. Although this is the most easily heard phoneme, children need to hear all the sounds in order to be able to write a word. They also need to be able to retain the phonemes in the right sequence in their working memory in order to spell the word. Skilled teaching supports them in this process. Phonics schemes today systematically introduce alternative phoneme to grapheme correspondences, giving children a range of spelling choices.

THE PLACE OF INVENTED SPELLING IN EARLY WRITING

The phrases 'invented spelling' and 'have a go spelling' describe the process whereby children make their own independent attempts at spelling words, rather than copying them, as was the approach in the past.

Invented spelling expects children to use their phonic knowledge and skills in an active and problem-solving approach to writing. Children using this approach tend to write and spell better (Gettinger, 1993).

ASSESSING PHONICS THROUGH SPELLING

The Year 1 phonics screening test only assesses children's reading – their ability to sound out and blend words. But we can learn a great deal about children's phonic skills and knowledge from their writing, and indeed we need to know whether they can segment words successfully and know appropriate graphemes to represent phonemes.

Consider this message written by Sophie, aged 6:

Dad	doonot	pant	the	wall	you	ideat	mum	stop	beaing	mean
mum	stop	lafing	at	me.						

Sophie is able to hear all the sounds in the words she writes (e.g. in 'idiot'). She hears the adjacent consonants in words such as 'paint' and 'stop'. She makes good attempts at long vowels in 'being' and 'do'. She is less successful with 'paint'.

Compare this with an extract from a letter by Grace, also aged 6:

Dear Shnona I thing theat the club is going not well a toll we ned mok pole.

Dear Shona, I think that the club is going not well at all. We need more people.

Grace represents phonemes that are not in the word (e.g. the first /n/ in 'Shona') and omits phonemes (e.g. the second /p/ in 'people'). Some spellings are bizarre (e.g. 'mok' for 'more') and she has difficulties with vowels (e.g. 'theat' for 'that' and 'ned' for 'need').

CLASSROOM ACTIVITIES

MAKE A WORD

This activity allows children to focus on segmenting words and matching graphemes to phonemes without needing to worry about letter formation.

RESOURCES

Sets of magnetic letters and boards, or a resource such as Phonix Cubes (cubes that have a grapheme written on them, and which can be clicked together to make words).

WHAT TO DO

Ask the children to make a word such as 'top'. Ask them to continue by making words such as 'tap', 'tip', 'tin', 'pin', 'pan', 'pat', 'sat' and 'sit'. Children may not realise they only need to change one grapheme each time and may feel more secure with the activity if they start afresh each time. There are many possible variations with this activity (e.g. using a series of words such as 'top', 'stop', 'stomp' or 'shot', 'shoot', 'shout', 'sheet').

SHARED WRITING

For children who are not yet writing independently, teacher modelling of phonics for writing is invaluable.

RESOURCES

Interactive whiteboard, whiteboard or flip chart, and a class set of 'keyboards' – laminated A4 cards with all the letters of the alphabet printed on them.

WHAT TO DO

Decide on a sentence to write, and repeat it, pointing to a finger for each word. Ask the children to repeat it together.

Say the first word clearly and ask the children to segment it orally. Ask the children to think about which letter is needed first and point to it on their 'keyboards'. Repeat until the word is complete and read the word back together. Ask the children for the next word and repeat the process until the whole sentence has been written.

If any word is used that includes phoneme–grapheme correspondences the children do not know yet, simply write it without discussion and tell the children what it says.

REFERENCE

Gettinger, M. (1993) Effects of invented spelling and direct instruction on spelling performance of second grade boys. *Journal of Applied Behaviour Analysis*, 26(3): 281–91.

FURTHER READING

Brien, J. (2012) *Teaching Primary English*. London: SAGE.

DfES (2007) *Letters and Sounds: Principles and Practice of High Quality Phonics*. London: DfES.

Johnston, R. and Watson, J. (2007) *Teaching Synthetic Phonics*. Exeter: Learning Matters.

Jolliffe, W., Waugh, D. and Gill, A. (2019) *Teaching Systematic Synthetic Phonics in Primary Schools* (3rd edition). London: SAGE.

Lewis, M. and Ellis, S. (eds) (2006) *Phonics Practice, Research and Policy*. London: SAGE.

Mudd, N. (1994) *Effective Spelling: A Practical Guide for Teachers*. London: Hodder & Stoughton.

O'Sullivan, O. and Thomas, A. (2007) *Understanding Spelling*. London: Routledge.

22

HOMOPHONES, HOMOGRAPHS AND HOMONYMS

WHAT DO I NEED TO KNOW?

HOMOPHONES

Homophones are words that sound the same but are spelled differently and have different meanings (e.g. 'grate' and 'great', 'weather' and 'whether', 'hole' and 'whole'). There are hundreds of these, and they can cause confusion when writers select the wrong word. Look at these examples:

I was given an exclusive peak at the first footage from the film.

The chairman was at fault for failing to reign in risk-taking.

His default look is fell-threw-a-hedge-backwards.

They stop to listen to the screams of another woman in the throws of a contraction.

The wool trade left behind in churches a fine stock of medieval knaves, chancels, windows and towers.

Smith was convicted of wreckless driving.

He smoked a cigar after diffusing the first bomb.

Everything was divided without a word of descent.

In all these cases, writers have selected not the wrong spelling but the wrong word, rather like using 'fortuitously' when 'fortunately' is meant, or 'disinterested' when 'uninterested' is meant, or 'reticent' for 'reluctant' (in these cases, the words are related, but different in structure and meaning). The spelling and meaning need to be clearly associated in the writer's mind to avoid these confusions.

HOMOGRAPHS

Homographs are words which are spelled the same but which sound different, as shown in the following examples:

The nurse wound the bandage carefully over the wound.

Our farm will now produce only organic produce.

The Council may refuse to remove your refuse.

I did not object to the object.

The insurance was invalid for the invalid.

These do not pose any particular difficulties for spelling, though they can trip up the unwary reader, who needs to use contextual clues to decide how to say the word.

HOMONYMS

Homonyms are words that have different meanings, and indeed have different origins, but which sound the same and are spelled the same. There are many of these: think, for example, of the different meanings of 'bear', 'bat', 'bark', 'bank', 'can', 'down', 'fine', 'fair', 'light', 'park', 'rock', 'rose', 'saw' and 'quarry'. These are important in vocabulary development but do not pose any difficulties for spelling. They are often the basis of children's jokes, such as:

Why did the cat come down from the tree? Because it saw the tree bark.

WHAT IS IT USEFUL TO KNOW?

HOMOPHONES AND ACCENT

Different accents often have different vowel phonemes in particular words (e.g. 'but' has a different vowel phoneme in northern areas from the one heard in the south of the country). Some pairs of words are therefore homophones in one accent but not in others. So, for some speakers, 'our' and 'are' are homophones; for other speakers, the two words sound very different. The same is true of 'won' and 'one', and 'none' and 'nun'.

There are far fewer differences in consonants in different accents, but many Irish and Scottish speakers use a phoneme that most English accents do not use at all at the beginning of words such as 'wheel', 'white' and 'when'. For these speakers, therefore, there is a clear difference between pairs such as 'which' and 'witch', which are homophones for other speakers. People may also hear pairs of words as homophones when spoken by someone with a different regional accent.

KEY KNOWLEDGE SUMMARY

WHAT ARE HOMOPHONES?

Words that sound the same as each other but are spelled differently.

WHAT ARE HOMOGRAPHS?

Words written the same but pronounced differently.

WHAT ARE HOMONYMS?

Words written and sounding identical, but with different meanings.

IN THE CLASSROOM

TEACHING THE SPELLING OF HOMOPHONES

It might seem obvious that homophones should be taught together, with clear explanations of the different word meanings (e.g. 'there', 'their' and 'they're') and warnings about the importance of not confusing them. However, this often seems to leave the message in children's minds that these are words which are easily confused, and as a result they do confuse them. Instead of teaching homophones together, therefore, they should be taught with words that share the same spelling pattern, and the meaning of the word in that context should be absolutely clear. For example:

- Teach 'there' with 'here' and 'where' – they are all words to do with location.

- Teach 'their' with 'heir' and an explanation that this is an unusual way of spelling the /air/ phoneme.

- Teach 'they're' in the context of contractions such as 'I'm', 'you're', 'he's', 'she's' and 'we're'.

- Teach 'lead' (the metal) with 'bread', 'instead' and 'head'. Children could write sentences such as 'My head was as heavy as lead' and 'The bread tasted like lead'.

- Teach 'led' (the verb, past tense) with 'fed', 'shed' and 'bed'. Children could write sentences such as 'I led the dog to its bed in the shed'.

- Teach 'pear' with 'pea' and 'peach' to link the spelling pattern to meaning, or with 'wear', 'bear' and 'tear' for links with sound and pattern.

- Teach 'pair' with 'fair', 'hair', 'stairs' and 'lair'. Children could write sentences such as 'I saw a pair of boys with fair hair'.

Good spellers are more likely to be able to compare homophones without confusing them, and may enjoy making collections of them.

USING GAMES AND WORKSHEETS

There are many games and worksheets available on the topic of homophones. However, they do not teach children how to decide on the correct alternative, and may even make the situation worse in that a child may become less sure about the correct spelling choice when faced with two or even three homophones. If the purpose is assessment rather than teaching, it is preferable to ask the child to write the target word, having heard it in a sentence so that the context is clear. From a diagnostic point of view, this will give more useful information, as is seen in the following example:

Target word: their

Children's incorrect attempts: there   thier   ther

Confusion of homophones is not the only issue here; there is also a misunderstanding of the phonemes that can be represented by the 'er' grapheme, and a misspelling that suggests either a misunderstanding of the 'i before e' rule or a tendency to reverse letter order.

HOMOGRAPHS IN THE CLASSROOM

Homographs are more relevant to reading than to writing. Faced with a word that could be pronounced in two different ways, only the context can guide the reader as to which is right. This is a particular issue when children know one word well – such as 'minute' – and then come across a sentence such as 'I saw a minute figure in the doorway'.

The learning point for children is that if they read something that sounds silly or doesn't make sense, they should check. Did they read it accurately? Could it be read in a different way that would make sense? Where graphemes can represent different phonemes (e.g. 'ow'), they need to learn:

It could be /ow/, it could be /oa/; if one way doesn't work, try the other.

HOMONYMS IN THE CLASSROOM

Vocabulary development is crucial to reading comprehension. When children are able to understand word play based on knowledge of homonyms (such as 'Why did the king draw straight lines? Because he was a ruler'), this is a marker of significant linguistic and cognitive development, as they are holding both meanings in their minds simultaneously.

Exploration of word meaning should be a regular part of classroom practice, not through dry exercises, but through discussion, investigation, browsing in dictionaries, thesauruses and joke books, and modelling of an interest in words by adults. The aim should be to ensure that every pupil develops the same interest in words as this 4-year-old, looking at a book with an adult:

Adult: *That's a robin.*

Child: *Robin – that's a funny word.*

Adult: *Why?*

Child: *Because my friend's called Robin, and he's not a bird.*

CLASSROOM ACTIVITIES

INVESTIGATING HOMONYMS

RESOURCES

Class set of dictionaries and word lists (homonyms such as 'back', 'bear', 'light' and 'fair').

WHAT TO DO

Give each group a different set of words to investigate. Ask the children first to write down any different meanings of each word they know, then to research the words in the dictionary to see if there are more meanings than the ones they were aware of. Collate the information on a wall chart.

HOMOGRAPH PAIRS

RESOURCES

List of common homographs (e.g. 'row', 'sow', 'tear', 'minute', 'wind', 'does', 'close', 'present'), examples of sentences containing homographs (e.g. 'The violinist put down his bow and took a bow'), and class set of dictionaries.

WHAT TO DO

Give the children a set of words and ask them to think of two ways of pronouncing each word, check they know the meaning of each homograph, using the dictionaries if necessary, and then invent a sentence using both words.

Collate the sentences on the board and reinforce the point that only context tells us the meaning of the word, and therefore how to say it.

FURTHER READING

Mudd, N. (1994) *Effective Spelling*. London: Hodder & Stoughton.

Roach, P. (1983) *English Phonetics and Phonology*. Cambridge: Cambridge University Press.

Schonell, F.J. (1957) *Essentials in Teaching and Testing Spelling*. London: Macmillan.

Waugh, D. and Jolliffe, W. (2017) *English 5–11: A Guide for Teachers*. London: Routledge.

Waugh, D., Warner, C. and Waugh, R. (2019) *Teaching Grammar, Punctuation and Spelling in Primary Schools* (3rd edition). London: SAGE.

23

PHRASES AND CLAUSES

WHAT DO I NEED TO KNOW?

In Chapter 24, you will see how sentences are made up of phrases and clauses. This chapter will look at those phrases and clauses in more detail.

A phrase is usually defined as 'a group of words which do a particular job in a sentence, but do not make sense on their own and do not contain a finite verb' (Melia, 2012, p27).

In contrast, a clause is a group of words that usually has a subject and a finite verb.

PHRASES

Phrases can theoretically consist of only one word, but usually there are two or more words that have a particular function within a sentence.

THE NOUN PHRASE (SEE CHAPTER 10)

Noun phrases can therefore be one noun (e.g. 'book') or two or more words with the function of a noun (e.g. 'exciting book').

Crystal (1996) describes a noun phrase as 'a string of words which all depend on the noun in some way. The noun is the most important word in a noun phrase. It tells you what the noun phrase is basically about' (p86).

The noun phrase can be the subject or object of the finite verb.

THE VERB PHRASE (SEE CHAPTER 11)

Similarly, in a verb phrase, the main function of the phrase is to act as a verb. The main word in a verb phrase is the verb preceded by one or more auxiliary verbs. A single-word example could be 'jumped', while a verb phrase with more than one word might be 'could have jumped'.

THE ADJECTIVAL PHRASE (SEE CHAPTER 12)

The adjectival phrase can, again, consist of one word (the adjective) or more than one word. The main adjective could be preceded by a modifying adverb (e.g. 'The tree was extremely old'). The final two words in this example make up the adjectival phrase.

THE ADVERBIAL PHRASE (SEE CHAPTER 13)

An adverbial phrase is a group of words that has the same function in a sentence as an adverb. In the sentence 'He ran quickly', 'quickly' is the adverb. This adverb can be replaced by the adverbial phrase 'extremely quickly'.

THE PREPOSITIONAL PHRASE (SEE CHAPTER 15)

A prepositional phrase contains a preposition that comes before a noun or a noun phrase. In the sentence 'The trees at the front of the garden are losing their leaves', 'at the front of the garden' gives the position of the noun 'trees'.

CLAUSES

As we saw at the beginning of this section, clauses, like phrases, are groups of words, but the difference lies in the fact that clauses contain a subject and a finite verb.

Main, or independent, clauses can stand on their own.

Subordinate, or dependent, clauses cannot stand on their own because they depend for their meaning on the main clause. A subordinate clause begins with a subordinating conjunction.

'Although Sarah skipped' contains a subject ('Sarah') and a finite verb ('skipped'), but because the clause begins with a conjunction ('although'), it does not make sense on its own. The reader would ask 'Although Sarah skipped – what?'

There are different types of subordinate clauses depending upon their function in the sentence.

THE NOUN CLAUSE (SEE CHAPTER 10)

In a complex sentence (see Chapter 23), a noun clause takes on the function of a noun. An example of this would be 'how kind you were to me' in the sentence 'I shall always remember how kind you were to me'.

THE ADJECTIVAL CLAUSE (SEE CHAPTER 12)

An adjectival clause describes a noun or pronoun in the main clause or sentence. An example of this would be 'which was a beautiful shade of red' in the sentence 'She wore a dress, which was a beautiful shade of red, to the party'.

Adjectival clauses often begin with 'that', 'who', 'which' or 'whom'.

THE ADVERBIAL CLAUSE (SEE CHAPTER 13)

An adverbial clause takes the place of an adverb, modifying a verb or an adjective. There are different types of adverbial clauses.

An example of an adverbial clause is 'when you are asleep' in the sentence 'Father Christmas comes when you are asleep'.

WHAT IS IT USEFUL TO KNOW?

As we saw above, there are different types of adverbial clauses. There is some disagreement as to the exact number of these clauses, but the most common are as follows.

CLAUSES OF PLACE

The clause often begins with the word 'where', describing where something was done (e.g. 'where the trees provided shade' in the sentence 'We had our picnic where the trees provided shade').

CLAUSES OF TIME

The clause often begins with the word 'when', describing when something happens (e.g. 'when you have finished your lunch' in the sentence 'You can have an ice cream when you have finished your lunch').

CLAUSES OF REASON

The clause often begins with the word 'because', describing why something happens (e.g. 'because it is cold' in the sentence 'I fastened my coat because it is cold').

CLAUSES OF PURPOSE

The clause often begins with the words 'so that', describing for what purpose something was done (e.g. 'so that I could hear clearly' in the sentence 'I sat at the front of the lecture room so that I could hear clearly').

CLAUSES OF CONDITION

The clause often begins with the word 'if', describing on what condition something would be done (e.g. 'If I have the time' in the sentence 'If I have the time, I will show you the garden').

CLAUSES OF CONCESSION

The clause often begins with the word 'although', asking 'despite what?' (e.g. 'Although he is only 2 years old' in the sentence 'Although he is only 2 years old, he can run across the room').

CLAUSES OF COMPARISON

There are two kinds of adverbial clauses of comparison: adverbial clauses of comparison of degree, and adverbial clauses of comparison of manner.

Adverbial clauses of comparison of degree often begin with the word 'than' and ask 'to what extent?' (e.g. 'than his sister' in the sentence 'John is younger than his sister').

Adverbial clauses of comparison of manner often begin with the word 'as' and describe how something is done (e.g. 'as well as I had hoped' in the sentence 'It did not work out as well as I had hoped').

Relative clauses give extra information about one of the nouns in the main clause. The beginning of a relative clause is usually marked by a relative pronoun (e.g. 'who', 'whose', 'which', 'that'). For example:

The boy who worked hard gained excellent marks in his exam.

In the above sentence, 'who worked hard' is the relative clause.

KEY KNOWLEDGE SUMMARY

Sentences are made up of clauses and phrases. Both are groups of words, but a clause has a subject and verb while a phrase does not. A clause can stand alone as a simple sentence (see Chapter 24) but a phrase cannot. In the sentence 'The boy is asleep on the bed', 'The boy is asleep' is a clause and has meaning, whereas 'on the bed' is a phrase because it has neither a subject nor a verb and does not make sense on its own.

IN THE CLASSROOM

In order to make their writing more interesting, children will be introduced to phrases and clauses that can expand a simple sentence. They will be taught that a phrase is a group of words without a verb while a clause is a group of words containing a subject and a main verb. As always, although some decontextualised exercises and activities can be interesting and give children the experience of addressing a particular grammatical point, it is always important to discuss phrases and clauses in the context of reading and writing.

PHRASES

Children may be taught that a phrase can be a single word, but that can be confusing, so, generally, they are taught that it is a group of words. They will learn that there are noun, adjectival, adverbial and prepositional phrases. A noun phrase has the function of a noun (see Chapter 10), an adjectival phrase the function of an adjective (see Chapter 12), an adverbial phrase the function of an adverb (see Chapter 13) and a prepositional phrase the function of a preposition (see Chapter 15).

Simple examples for children to understand are as follows.

NOUN PHRASE

I ate an ice cream. ('ice cream' is a noun)

I ate an ice cream cornet. ('ice cream cornet' is a noun phrase, giving us a little more information)

ADJECTIVAL PHRASE

The school outing was exciting. ('exciting' is an adjective)

The school outing was really exciting and interesting. ('really exciting and interesting' is an adjectival phrase)

ADVERBIAL PHRASE

Surprisingly, the concert was cancelled. ('Surprisingly' is an adverb)

Rather surprisingly, the concert was cancelled. ('Rather surprisingly' is an adverbial phrase)

PREPOSITIONAL PHRASE

He hid the treasure behind the tree. ('behind' is a preposition)

He hid the treasure behind the tree in the neighbour's garden. ('behind the tree in the neighbour's garden' is a prepositional phrase)

CLAUSES

Children will learn that there are two types of clause: main or independent clauses, and subordinate or dependent clauses.

Independent clauses can act as sentences, but dependent clauses cannot, and it is important that children recognise the difference between the two types. Often children will write a dependent clause and think that because there is a subject and a main verb, then that clause is a sentence and can stand alone. For example, the clause 'because he ate all of his lunch' has a subject ('he') and a main or finite verb ('ate'), and children may think that the clause can be a complete sentence. The easiest way to address this is to ask: Does it make sense? What happened 'because he ate all of his lunch'?

If we need to say more to children about subordinate clauses, we can divide them into different categories by looking at what job they are doing in a sentence.

In the National Curriculum (DfE, 2013), it is part of the statutory requirements at the end of Key Stage 1 that pupils should learn how to use:

- *expanded noun phrases to describe and specify (for example, the blue butterfly);*

- *subordination (using when, if, that or because) and co-ordination (using or, and, or but).*

(p32)

At the end of Key Stage 2, the statutory requirements for grammar include that pupils should be taught:

- *[to use] expanded noun phrases to convey complicated information concisely;*

- *[to use] relative clauses beginning with who, which, where, when, whose, that or with an implied (i.e. omitted) relative pronoun.*

(p48)

Note: Relative clauses are dependent clauses that are introduced by relative pronouns such as 'which', 'that', 'who' and so on.

The term 'fronted adverbials' has caused a little stir with primary teachers preparing to teach the National Curriculum with its appearance in the glossary (DfE, 2013). Its meaning is fairly straight-forward. An adverbial is a word, phrase or clause that is used to modify a verb. 'Fronted' simply means that it is at the front of a sentence. An example of this is the adverbial clause 'Before I go out to play' in the sentence 'Before I go out to play, I must finish my homework'.

The practice of shared writing, in which the teacher models and edits the writing of the whole class together, is very effective for teaching children about phrases and clauses. This collaborative writing allows the teacher to demonstrate good practice, address misconceptions and assess children's understanding. Oral rehearsing, or 'talk for writing', is an important part of the process. Because the teacher is acting as scribe, the children can offer their ideas without worrying about the transcriptional aspects of the writing. Myhill (2010) describes how the concept of 'cognitive overload' is very relevant to children's writing process because writing makes great demands on working memory:

Having to pay attention to handwriting, word spacing and spelling means that young writers have little or no working memory available to think about other aspects of writing, such as what they want to say and how they might say it.

(p6)

Explicit teaching of grammatical terms has recently come back into favour. Not everyone agrees that being familiar with linguistic terminology will improve children's writing (e.g. Hillocks, 1986; Carter, 1990). However, in interactive shared writing, being able to use terminology can enhance the discussion. In the National Curriculum (DfE, 2013), the non-statutory guidance for Key Stage 1 suggests that:

The terms for discussing language should be embedded for pupils in the course of discussing their writing with them. Their attention should be drawn to the technical terms they need to learn.

(p32)

Similarly, at the end of Key Stage 2, the non-statutory guidance suggests that:

Pupils should continue to add to their knowledge of linguistic terms, including those to describe grammar, so that they can discuss their reading and writing.

(p48)

When talking about the use of phrases and clauses, it is important that the children are aware of the reader so that their writing is purposeful. For example, children will be asked such questions as:

How can we make this simple sentence more interesting to a reader?

Can you think of a phrase that will make readers of this story learn more about the character?

We know the girl wore a new dress, but can we extend the adjective 'new' by using an adjectival clause to make it more interesting and informative?

CLASSROOM ACTIVITIES

EXPANDING NOUN PHRASES

Children will demonstrate their understanding of noun phrases.

RESOURCES

Individual whiteboards and whiteboard pens.

WHAT TO DO

Ask the children, as a whole class, to consider the following noun phrases:

a red rose

a bright, red rose

a perfumed, bright, red rose

Ask them to create, on their whiteboards, similar expanded phrases for the following examples:

a pet dog

a sunny day

a blue dress

Ask the children to swap their boards with a response partner and ask their partners to change a noun phrase on one line in each of the examples.

PHRASES OR CLAUSES?

Children will learn to differentiate between phrases and clauses.

RESOURCES

Whiteboard, and individual whiteboards and whiteboard pens.

WHAT TO DO

Explain to the children the difference between a phrase and a clause.

Ask them to consider the following examples and decide whether they are phrases or clauses. Do the words tell you what is happening? Is there a verb?

A very large dog

The dog went for a walk

A sunny day

The sun shone

The monkey in the zoo

The monkey jumped from branch to branch

It is important to discuss the children's responses to assess their understanding.

Then ask the children to write a group of words on their individual whiteboards and ask their response partners to say whether their words make up a phrase or a clause.

Again, these examples should be discussed with the whole group in a shared writing session.

CREATING SENTENCES

Children will create sentences using independent and dependent clauses.

RESOURCES

Strips of paper divided into two sets. One set will have written on each strip the beginning of a sentence, an independent clause. The other set will have written on each strip the ending of a sentence, a dependent clause.

WHAT TO DO

Organise the children into pairs.

One child in each pair will be given strips of paper, each containing a main, independent clause.

The other child in each pair will be given strips of paper, each containing a subordinate, dependent clause.

The first child chooses a piece of paper and puts it in the middle of the table.

The second child completes the sentence with an appropriate dependent clause.

Examples:

Independent clauses	*Dependent clauses*
He got ready for bed	*after I had finished my supper.*
The dog was barking	*while Josephine sang.*
I cleaned my teeth	*although it was not yet bedtime.*
James played the piano	*because there was someone at the door.*
Owen is good at art	*before she could bake the cake.*
Ann needed more flour	*whereas Paul is good at PE.*

REFERENCES

Carter, R. (ed.) (1990) *Knowledge about Language and the Curriculum: The LINC Reader*. London: Hodder & Stoughton.

Crystal, D. (1996) *Discover Grammar*. Harlow: Addison Wesley Longman.

DfE (2013) *The National Curriculum*. London: DfE.

Hillocks, G. (1986) *Research in Written Composition: New Directions for Teaching*. Urbana, IL: ERIC & NCTE.

Melia, S. (2012) *The Primary Teacher's Guide to Grammar and Punctuation*. Witney: Scholastic.

Myhill, D. (2010) 'Learning to write', in R. Fisher, D. Myhill, S. Jones and S. Larkin (eds), *Using Talk to Support Writing*. London: SAGE.

FURTHER READING

Corbett, P. and Strong, J. (2011) *Talk for Writing across the Curriculum*. Maidenhead: Open University Press.

Pollock, J. and Waller, E. (1999) *English Grammar and Teaching Strategies*. London: David Fulton.

Watson, K. (2003) *Succeed in English*. London: Arcturus Publishing.

Waugh, D. Warner, C. and Waugh, R. (2019) *Teaching Grammar, Spelling and Punctuation in Primary Schools*. London: Learning Matters.

24

SENTENCES

WHAT DO I NEED TO KNOW?

A sentence is a set of words that contains a subject and a predicate. The subject is the topic of the sentence (i.e. what the sentence is about). The predicate is what the subject does. The predicate must always contain a verb; in fact, it may consist only of the verb. The predicate may also include the object of the verb:

The dog chewed the bone.

In this sentence, 'the dog' is the subject and 'chewed the bone' is the predicate because it tells us what the dog did; 'chewed' is the verb and 'the bone' is the object of the verb.

I am.

In this very short sentence, 'I' is the subject and 'am' is the predicate and the all-important verb. You will notice that the predicate, in this case, has no object.

There are three types of sentence:

1. simple;

2. compound; and

3. complex.

To understand the difference between the different types of sentence, you need more information.

First of all, you need to know the definition and function of clauses and phrases (see Chapter 23).

A simple sentence consists of a subject and a predicate:

The girl kicked the ball.

A compound sentence consists of two clauses joined together by a coordinating conjunction (e.g. 'and', 'or', 'but', 'nor', 'so', 'for', 'yet'):

The dog barked and the cat ran.

Lucy was playing yet she was not happy.

Each clause could be a simple sentence as it has a subject and predicate.

A complex sentence consists of a main (independent) clause and one or more subordinate (dependent) clauses. For example:

While the music played, the children danced around the room.

'The children danced around the room' is the main clause because this is what the sentence is mainly about. 'While the music played' is supporting the main clause, and is therefore subordinate to it (i.e. simply giving additional information). 'While' is a subordinating conjunction. Other examples of subordinate conjunctions are 'however', 'because', 'although', 'after', 'until', 'before' and 'since'.

Note: Where the main (independent) clause is at the beginning of the sentence, it does not need to be followed by a comma, but where the subordinate (dependent) clause is at the beginning of the sentence, this does need a comma, as in the example above.

Sentences have different functions.

Declarative sentences (e.g. statements):

I love reading.

Interrogative sentences (e.g. questions or requests):

Why is the boy jumping over the hedge?

Imperative sentences (e.g. commands or instructions):

Do your homework now.

Exclamative sentences (e.g. for exclamations):

I can't believe it!

Remember, all sentences begin with capital letters. Sentences end with a full stop, a question mark or an exclamation mark (see examples above).

WHAT IS IT USEFUL TO KNOW?

We use sentences when writing but not always when speaking. 'Utterance' is the term used for spoken language. When speaking, we do not always speak in a considered, grammatically correct way, and this is entirely appropriate. There are often a few 'ums' and 'ers' (filled pauses), false starts and unintentional repetition. Body language is also used to help convey meaning.

The following examples show first how we may speak and second how we write:

I suppose youre er going to um have your ... tea later

I suppose you are going to have your tea later.

Yknow I dont think that we need to em like do that

I do not think that we need to do that.

I think you could have – you should have been there

I think you should have been there.

Crystal (1996) describes how, in speech, the rhythm and tune of the voice replaces punctuation (e.g. rising intonation when asking a question).

When writing, there is time to organise thoughts and redraft text to communicate most effectively. In written text, punctuation, as boundary markers, is very important (see Chapter 25).

KEY KNOWLEDGE SUMMARY

To convey meaning, it is important to write in sentences. A sentence should contain a subject and a verb. Sentences begin with a capital letter and end with a full stop, a question mark or an exclamation mark. Ensure that you read Chapter 23. A simple sentence consists of a single clause with one subject and one main verb:

The dog ate the biscuit.

A compound sentence has two main clauses joined by a conjunction (e.g. 'and' or 'but'):

The dog ate a biscuit but he left his water.

A complex sentence consists of a main clause and a subordinate clause. The subordinate clause needs the main clause to make sense:

Although he had just had a big dinner, the dog ate a biscuit.

IN THE CLASSROOM

Young children begin their written communication by scribbling on a page. It has long been recognised that these scribbles are logical and not haphazard (Ferreiro and Teberosky, 1979). Bunting (2003) describes how children's emergent writing, their scribbles, can be 'patiently and painstakingly constructed communications, as children learn both that language is a symbolic system for expressing meaning and that it has rules of usage' (p10). The children learn that in English, they write from left to right; this is not the case in all languages.

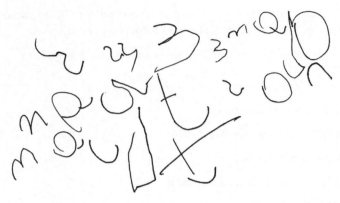

Figure 24.1   This is an example of Madison's first writing, where she has learned to write from left to right, and she has included some letters (particularly from her name) and the occasional number for good measure.

Gradually, the children will write letters and simple words.

Figure 24.2   Here, Isabella has written about a princess: 'The princess had a rabbit. She loved the guinea pig. She had a beautiful dress'.

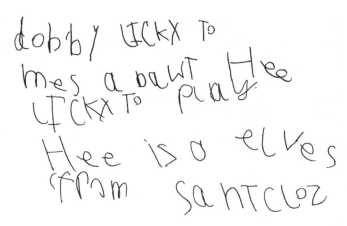

Figure 24.3   Luke has written, 'Dobby likes to mess about. He likes to play. He is an elf from Santa Claus'.

The next stage is for them to organise their words into complete sentences and understand how important this is for communication.

Younger pupils are usually taught that a sentence is a group of words that makes sense. So, if you write 'The boy', you would want to know what the boy did (e.g. 'kicked' – the verb) and perhaps what was kicked (e.g. 'the ball' – the object). Similarly, if you write 'went to the park', you would want to know who went to the park (the subject). The first activities in this chapter will help develop children's understanding of complete sentences.

Kelly (2003) describes how children develop an implicit understanding of sentences, even complex sentences. In early writing, punctuation might not always be correct, but the structure of the sentence is often recognisable.

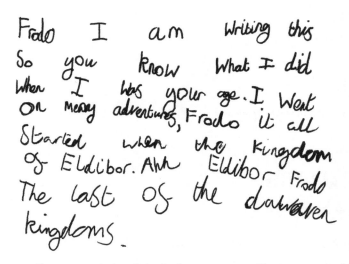

Figure 24.4   Joshua is beginning to structure his sentences in this piece of writing.

It will be important to explicitly discuss different written genres where complete sentences are not required. For example, the children will read and write poetry, where normal sentence structure may not create the best effect. Similarly, headlines will not necessarily be written in complete sentences.

For examples of poetry where normal sentence structure has been discarded, look at those of E.E. Cummings: **http://poems.writers-network.com/ee_cummings**

The purpose of headlines is to grab the reader's attention. Sentences would be unwieldy and so a telegraphic style is often used:

Blazing Inferno

Rat Epidemic

Red Hot August

Children need lots of experience of different text types. Genre is an important consideration when we think of length and complexity of sentences. In instructional text, for example, simple, direct sentences are generally more effective. In a narrative text, however, variety is usually more dynamic. Once children have mastered the complex sentence, it might be very tempting for them to use one after the other in their own writing. Lots of examples from books should be used to demonstrate the importance of variety. Again, this will have to be explicitly discussed.

Examples of simple sentences for instructional text might include a recipe:

Making Scrambled Eggs

Heat oil or knob of butter in a pan.

Take three eggs.

Crack them into a bowl.

Add a little milk.

Add salt and pepper.

Whisk briskly.

Pour mixture into pan.

Stir continuously using a wooden spoon.

Enjoy.

CLASSROOM ACTIVITIES
COMPLETING SENTENCES (1)

Children sort cards into sentences and non-sentences.

RESOURCES

Strips of laminated card.

WHAT TO DO

Before the lesson, prepare the cards, some with sentences written on them and some with only fragments (non-sentences) on them.

Ask the children to arrange the cards into a pile of sentences and non-sentences.

COMPLETING SENTENCES (2)

Children find their 'sentence partner' to complete the sentence.

RESOURCES

Laminated card.

WHAT TO DO

Before the lesson, write out simple sentences on laminated card. Cut the cards into subject and predicate sections.

Give each child a section of a sentence (subject or predicate). Ask them to walk round the room until they meet someone who has the section that will complete their sentence. The sentence would have to make sense in meaning as well as grammatically.

Shuffle the cards and repeat the activity.

VARIATIONS

With older children, compound sentences could be cut up into three parts: two independent clauses and a conjunction. Again, the sentences would need to make sense, including an appropriate conjunction.

SENTENCE DETECTIVES

Build up a collection of different types of sentences.

RESOURCES

Notebooks (optional).

WHAT TO DO

Encourage the children to spot different types of sentences when they are reading their books. This can work by spotting simple, compound and complex sentences or examples of declarative, interrogative, exclamative or imperative sentences. Over time, the children can build up collections of sentences in special notebooks and share these during whole-class sessions. Alternatively, you may want to create a classroom area where the children display examples they find.

CONSEQUENCES

Learning that sentences may be grammatically correct but still not make sense.

RESOURCES

Pen and paper.

WHAT TO DO

The children work in pairs.

Each child writes the subject of a sentence on a piece of paper then folds the paper over from left to right, leaving the last letter visible.

The paper is passed over to the other child, who completes the sentence by writing a verb and an object (i.e. the predicate).

This can be completed several times. The children will see that the sentences may make sense grammatically but may result in very amusing outcomes!

VARIETY

Encouraging a variety of sentence types to write interesting texts.

RESOURCES

Pen and paper.

WHAT TO DO

Ask the children to write a short narrative passage that contains only simple sentences.

Then ask them to rewrite the text using at least one simple sentence, one compound sentence and one complex sentence. Each type of sentence could be written or highlighted in a different colour.

Discussion should follow that compares the different written texts and their respective effectiveness.

REFERENCES

Bunting, R. (2003) 'From process to genre to strategy: recent developments in the teaching of writing', in J. Graham and A. Kelly (eds), *Writing under Control* (2nd edition). Chiswick: David Fulton.

Crystal, D. (1996) *Discover Grammar*. London: Longman.

Ferreiro, E. and Teberosky, A. (1979) *Literacy before Schooling*. London: Heinemann.

Kelly, A. (2003) 'Transcription: spelling, punctuation and handwriting', in J. Graham and A. Kelly (eds), *Writing under Control* (2nd edition). Chiswick: David Fulton.

FURTHER READING

Waugh, D., Warner, C. and Waugh, R. (2013) *Teaching Grammar, Punctuation and Spelling in Primary Schools* (3rd edition). London: SAGE, Chapter 8.

USEFUL WEBSITES

For 'Gangnam Style' types of sentences, see **www.youtube.com/watch/v=AFGs3oT7nQg**

Grammar for Writing was published to provide teaching and learning ideas and activities for the Literacy Framework. Although this has now been superseded by the National Curriculum, it still provides a wealth of useful material. See **www.schoolslinks.co.uk/GrammarForWriting.pdf**

25

PARAGRAPHS

WHAT DO I NEED TO KNOW?

PARAGRAPHS

Long texts are usually divided into paragraphs. Each paragraph will consist of sentences that are connected or sometimes just one long sentence. Most paragraphs begin with a topic sentence. This topic sentence is then elaborated in the later sentences in the paragraph. The following paragraph may develop the previous paragraph's elaboration or may introduce a different topic/point. In moving from one paragraph to another, it is helpful to use linking words or phrases (e.g. 'however', 'therefore', 'in addition', 'consequently', 'despite this fact').

THE LENGTH OF PARAGRAPHS

Paragraphs may be short or long; they can be just one sentence (which itself may be short or long). Paragraphs may indeed be as short as one word. Where a paragraph has only one sentence, this has the effect of drawing the reader's attention to it, and writers will do this for emphasis.

An example of this is the following one-sentence paragraph taken from John McGregor's *Even the Dogs*:

> They cut his body open in a clean white room and take him apart piece by piece.

A one-sentence paragraph is more likely to appear in a novel or magazine article than in academic writing.

Good, organised and coherent paragraphing helps the reader to follow the writing, while poorly organised paragraphs will confuse or even lose the reader. Coherence (all sentences should be related to the topic) and development are crucial.

There should be a logical and natural close to the paragraph.

NEW PARAGRAPHS

When writing narrative, a new paragraph is usually used when a new event or character is introduced or when there is a change of place or time. This last point is illustrated in the following example, taken from Hilary Mantel's *Wolf Hall*:

They are taking apart the cardinal's house. Room by room, the king's men are stripping York palace of its owner. They are bundling up parchments and scrolls, missals and memoranda and the volumes of his personal accounts; they are taking even the ink and quills. They are prising from the walls the boards on which the cardinal's coat of arms is painted.

They arrived on a Sunday, two vengeful grandees: the Duke of Norfolk, a bright-eyed hawk, the Duke of Suffolk just as keen. They told the cardinal he was dismissed as Lord Chancellor and demanded he hand over the Great Seal of England. Etc.

In dialogue, each speaker is usually given a new line, a new paragraph, even if the utterance is short. Another example from *Wolf Hall*:

Lizzie is still up. When she hears the servants let him in, she comes out with her little dog under her arm, fighting and squealing.

'Forget where you lived?'

He sighs.

'How was Yorkshire?'

He shrugs.

'The cardinal?'

He nods.

'Eaten?'

'Yes.'

'Tired?'

'Not really.'

'Drink?'

'Yes.'

'Rhenish?'

'Why not.'

WHAT IS IT USEFUL TO KNOW?

The word 'paragraph' comes from the Greek *paragraphos*, 'to write beside' or 'written beside'. In a paragraph, we know that sentences are written beside one another in sequence.

GRAPHOLOGY

The graphology (layout) of paragraphs has a visual impact on the reader. Each new paragraph begins on a new line, either indenting or leaving a blank line (or both). There is no hard and fast rule, but you should be consistent.

NEWSPAPERS AND MAGAZINES

In newspapers, after the headline, which draws attention to the story, there is the first paragraph, which is known as the lead paragraph. This paragraph summarises and begins the story.

An example of a lead paragraph includes:

Blue badges for people with hidden disabilities

People with less visible disabilities such as dementia and anxiety can now apply to use blue badge parking permits, the Government has announced.

(i weekend, 2019, p4)

The article goes on to discuss further details in other paragraphs that vary in length.

KEY KNOWLEDGE SUMMARY

Paragraphs break up larger pieces of text so that writing is easier to read and understand. A paragraph consists of a sentence or group of sentences that have the same theme. Often each paragraph will contain a topic sentence that introduces the theme of the paragraph.

IN THE CLASSROOM

Children need to know that longer texts are organised into paragraphs consisting of sentences that relate to a particular topic. In narrative writing, a new paragraph is usually used when a new character, event or place is introduced. Consider the following extract from Tove Jansson's *Finn Family Moomintroll*, for example:

One grey morning the first snow began to fall in the Valley of the Moomins. It fell softly and quietly, and in a few hours everything was still.

Moomintroll stood on his doorstep and watched the valley nestle beneath its winter blanket. 'Tonight', he thought, 'we shall settle down for our long winter's sleep'.

FIRST PARAGRAPHS

The first paragraph describes the beautiful setting and then a new paragraph is begun to introduce the main character and the beginning of the story.

REPORT WRITING

In report writing, each paragraph usually addresses a different point related to the main topic. The first sentence of each paragraph often tells the reader what the paragraph is going to be about, and is called the 'key' or 'topic' sentence.

WRITING FRAMES

'Writing frames' are outlines or templates that guide children to write in a particular genre. They are particularly useful when introducing non-fiction genres where the text type may require particular structures and language. Writing frames are also very useful in the teaching of the importance of paragraphs. For example, a frame could be used to introduce the children to the writing of persuasive text. A structure and keywords are provided, and the children have to write appropriate paragraphs. Here, for example, is a writing frame to support children in the writing of persuasive text:

I believe that it is wrong to …

Some people might say that …

However, on looking at the facts, I think that …

In conclusion, I would like to say that …

Under each heading, the children should be encouraged to write a paragraph.

It is always important to remember that children should move on to independent writing as quickly as possible; writing frames should just offer initial support.

The idea of supporting (or scaffolding) children in this way comes from the work of Vygotsky (1978), who described how children move from needing a lot of support when initially beginning a task to gradually needing less and less supervision until they can complete a task on their own.

CLASSROOM ACTIVITIES

PARAGRAPH DETECTIVES

Children will search their books for paragraphs.

RESOURCES

A selection of books.

WHAT TO DO

The children will become 'paragraph detectives'.

In pairs, they will look through a number of books and discuss with their partners what each paragraph is about and why the writer has begun a new paragraph.

STORYBOARDS

Children divide a story into topic pictures to develop an understanding of paragraphs.

RESOURCES

Paper, pencils and crayons, and a short story to read to the children.

WHAT TO DO

Read a short story to the children.

Ask the children, as a class, to pick out the main parts of the story.

Tell them to draw a picture for each part of the story (creating a storyboard). This part is to be carried out individually.

Ask them to write underneath each picture a sentence describing the picture.

Finally, ask the children to write one or two more sentences under each picture to expand on the main sentence to create a paragraph.

Discuss what the children have done with the whole class, describing how they have created paragraphs.

WRITING FRAME (1)

The teacher will model the use of a frame for writing a discussion.

RESOURCES

A flip chart or interactive whiteboard with the following writing frame set out:

We are going to discuss …

We have been arguing about whether or not …

Some people think that …

On the other hand, others of us think that …

In conclusion …

WHAT TO DO

A topic is chosen that the class have recently been discussing (e.g. the wearing of school uniform).

The teacher works with the class to produce a paragraph for each section.

WRITING FRAME (2)

Children will write their own discussions based on the earlier modelled lesson.

RESOURCES

Worksheets with the following set out:

We are going to discuss …

We have been arguing about whether or not …

Some people think that …

On the other hand, others of us think that …

In conclusion …

WHAT TO DO

A different topic may be chosen from the one discussed with the whole class, or the same topic could be used.

The children should be encouraged to write a paragraph for each section.

REFERENCES

i weekend (2019) 'Blue badges for people with hidden disabilities'. *i weekend*, 15–16 June, p4.

Jansson, T. (1948) *Finn Family Moomintroll*. Middlesex: Puffin Books.

Mantel, H. (2009) *Wolf Hall*. London: Fourth Estate.

McGregor, J. (2010) *Even the Dogs*. London: Bloomsbury.

Vygotsky, L. (1978) *Minds in Society*. Cambridge, MA: Harvard University Press.

FURTHER READING

Graff, R. (2011) *Instant Nonfiction Writing*. London: Scholastic.

Wray, D. and Lewis, M. (1997) *Extending Literacy*. London: Routledge.

USEFUL WEBSITE

A short video quiz for children can be found at **www.bbc.co.uk/bitesize/ks2/english/ spelling_grammar/paragraphs/play/**

26

PUNCTUATION

WHAT DO I NEED TO KNOW?

Punctuation is the use of graphic marks in written texts that help clarify meaning.

Punctuation marks include:

- *capital letters at the beginning of sentences;*

- *full stops at the end of sentences;*

- *question marks at the end of sentences which are questions; and*

- *apostrophes to mark elision (don't) and possession (John's).*

(Bunting, 1997, p44)

Punctuation can help avoid ambiguities in a text as well as change the meaning of a sentence. The sentences below, for example, have very different meanings:

She likes cooking, dogs and children.

She likes cooking dogs and children.

Some aspects of punctuation are more open to personal preference. These are less prescriptive (conventions rather than rules), and include exclamation marks, commas, colons, semicolons and brackets.

EXAMPLES OF PUNCTUATION MARKS
FULL STOP (.)

This is used to signal the end of a sentence (typically a statement):

I am going home now.

It is also used to mark an abbreviated word (e.g. etc.) and times and dates (e.g. 9.25, 16.8.13).

COLON (:)

This is used mainly to show that what follows the colon is an explanation, illustration or expansion of what has preceded it. The clause that precedes the colon should be able to stand as an independent clause:

We had to cancel the meeting: too many people were unable to attend.

The colon is also used to introduce a list:

To make bread, you need the following ingredients: flour, yeast, salt and water.

SEMICOLON (;)

This is used to join two main clauses in a single sentence. The semicolon must be preceded by a clause and followed by a clause that relates to the first. The relationship between the two clauses is made clear by use of the semicolon. The semicolon can, in principle, be replaced by a full stop to produce two separate sentences, or joined by words such as 'and', 'but' or 'yet':

John went to Paris for his holidays; Sarah stayed at home.

COMMA (,)

The comma is the most frequently used punctuation mark and with the greatest use of personal variation. It marks a sequence of similar grammatical units (words, phrases, clauses) in a sentence.

An example of separating a series of words is:

I went to the shop and bought bread, milk, cereal and chocolate.

Note that there is no comma before the final 'and'.

An example of using a comma to separate phrases is:

At weekends I enjoy a long walk, a coffee with friends and a browse in a bookshop.

An example of using a comma to separate clauses is:

I went to Prague, Keith went to New York, Rosie went to Stockholm and Tom went to Rome.

QUESTION MARK (?)

This comes at the end of a sentence asking a question and replacing a full stop:

What time are we meeting on Tuesday?

EXCLAMATION MARK (!)

This punctuation mark is often used where strong emotions are expressed. It replaces the full stop:

Great goal!

Get down from there!

INVERTED COMMAS (' ' OR " ")

Also known as quotation marks or speech marks, these indicate direct speech or an extract cited from another text:

Tommy said, 'Tomorrow evening I'm hoping to go to the party'.

Note that there is a comma before the beginning of the direct speech and that the first letter within the speech marks is capitalised:

'Tomorrow evening I'm hoping to go to the party', said Tommy, 'after I've finished work'.

Note that in this example, what has actually been said is broken up, and here a comma is required after the first part of the utterance and again after the person speaking; the second part of the utterance does not begin with a capital letter.

It is perfectly correct to use either version of speech marks; you can use single inverted commas or double inverted commas. The important thing is to be consistent in your use. Whichever choice you make, if there is speech within speech or a quotation used within speech, use the other version for this part of the text.

BRACKETS ( )

Also called parentheses, these are an alternative to commas. Brackets are used where subordinate information is added in such a way that the flow of the sentence is not interrupted. The sentence without the brackets should make grammatical sense:

The flowers (particularly the roses) are beautiful this year.

DASH (–)

This mark is used in pairs to mark off information or ideas that are not essential to understanding the rest of the sentence. What is included in between the dashes is the additional information:

My daughter – who is 10 – would like to go to the cinema.

ELLIPSIS (...)

An ellipsis is a set of, usually, three dots that indicates the omission of words, phrases or clauses from a sentence where the ellipted elements are implied or can be understood from the context.

We could do that ... or maybe ...

Oh, if only I had ... I suppose it doesn't matter now.

APOSTROPHE (')

An apostrophe can mark grammatical contractions (e.g. 'can't', 'wouldn't'). Here, the apostrophe is used to denote where a letter (or letters) is missing. It is also used to denote possession (e.g. 'the girl's book', 'the boys' toys'). Notice the placement of the apostrophe in words that are plurals. There is much to say about the apostrophe, so a whole chapter is dedicated to it (see Chapter 27).

WHAT IS IT USEFUL TO KNOW?

The system of punctuation used today is the result of many changes over the centuries. Early classical texts did not use punctuation and did not have spaces between words. In later times, and particularly with the invention of printing, around 1476, when Caxton set up his press in Westminster, standardisation gradually emerged. This change was very slow, however, and punctuation in Shakespeare's works, for example, was very idiosyncratic. In the eighteenth century, punctuation began to resemble how it looks today, although differences from modern day continued until well into the nineteenth century.

Hall (1996) describes how punctuation 'is sensitive to stylistic change' (p10). Punctuation does not have the same degree of rules that govern grammar and spelling, and is to some extent a matter of personal preference. We may use a dash or parentheses in place of a comma. Another example is the use of single or double inverted commas to indicate direct speech or quotations from a text. Both are correct, and the choice of which to use differs from person to person and among publishers.

Punctuation is, however, necessary to mark boundaries between grammatical constructions (i.e. units of language – phrases, clauses and sentences). It also marks status. For example, is the sentence a question or a statement? Is the sentence indicating the use of direct speech? Is a character shouting or excited? In speech, this is achieved through prosody (i.e. intonation, pitch, volume, pace and rhythm) and paralinguistic features (i.e. non-verbal communication – gestures, facial expression and posture).

In spoken language, it is easy to clarify meaning quickly as most speech is face to face or in telephone conversations. Written texts need punctuation to ensure clarification.

KEY KNOWLEDGE SUMMARY

Punctuation is important in that it ensures that the writer conveys the intended meaning. It consists of signs such as full stops, commas and question marks that show how a text should be read. The well-known sentences below demonstrate just how important commas are:

Let's eat grandma.

Let's eat, grandma.

IN THE CLASSROOM

Children need to be taught that punctuation is important for the understanding of texts. Waugh and Jolliffe (2017) maintain:

> We require punctuation when we write so that we can compensate for the lack of intonation that is possible in speech. However, punctuation can be a matter of style and some people make greater use of commas, hyphens and exclamation marks than others in order to achieve a certain effect upon the reader.
>
> Punctuation marks enable us to define the status of the sentences we write. Through their use we can indicate whether a sentence is a question, a statement or direct speech, and whether a speaker is exclaiming.

(p77)

Here, an awareness of audience is stressed, and as children develop that awareness they will recognise the need for punctuation both as readers and as writers. Kelly (2010) talks about the importance of children having a sense of audience when writing. If they have a reader in mind, then they are more likely to realise that punctuation is there to help the reader's understanding.

However, learning to use punctuation is not straightforward; one of the main difficulties is that children do not easily understand the unit that is the sentence. For example, a head teacher spoke to parents about the requirements of the very first Key Stage 1 writing standard assessment task (SAT), one of them being to write in sentences, clearly demarcated with full stops and capital letters. The next time their children produced a piece of writing at school, every line of writing was marked with a full stop as big as a lollipop. The children had no sense of a sentence, but they were certainly going to produce the biggest full stops ever seen!

Discussion about punctuation is very important. Whenever possible, attention should be drawn to children's books and the punctuation used. Guided reading and writing sessions are particularly useful times for discussion: What does that question mark tell you? What about that exclamation mark? How would you read the sentence if it wasn't there? Children should be encouraged to read their own written texts aloud as often as possible so that the need for punctuation can be discussed. We expect children to read with more intonation as their reading develops. This is certainly the time to recognise punctuation in their reading of books and use punctuation for effect in their own writing. It is important, as with all learning, to build on what children already know rather than bombarding them with rules.

As was shown earlier, children need to know that there is a reason for punctuation, that communication and audience are important, and teachers need to discuss those reasons with their pupils in reading and writing sessions.

CLASSROOM ACTIVITIES

PUNCTUATION DETECTIVES

Children will discover that there are marks in their books. At this early stage, the function of those marks will not be important.

RESOURCES

Coloured pencils, a range of percussion instruments, and copies of simple poems or nursery rhymes written on large sheets of paper. The poems should be chosen for the variety of punctuation used.

This rhyme contains commas, a question mark, exclamation marks, an apostrophe and a full stop:

> *The north wind doth blow,*
>
> *And we shall have snow,*
>
> *And what will poor robin do then?*
>
> *Poor thing!*
>
> *He'll sit in a barn,*
>
> *And keep himself warm,*
>
> *And hide his head under his wing.*
>
> *Poor thing!*

WHAT TO DO

The children should work in small groups.

Each group should be given a different rhyme.

Within each group, the children should 'detect' all the different punctuation marks. It is not important at this stage that they know the names of the punctuation marks.

Each different mark should be given a different percussion instrument and each child assigned to that instrument and punctuation mark. So, for example, one child in the group will be the full stop and bang a drum.

All of the children in the group should read out the poem, with the relevant child playing his/her instrument when the punctuation mark occurs. For example, Sophie might play a tambourine every time there is a comma, while Simon plays the drum when there is a full stop.

Each group could perform to the whole class.

It is important to remember that at this early stage, the children are just being alerted to the marks, to simply notice that they are there.

DISCUSSING PUNCTUATION

Children will begin to understand the function of different punctuation marks.

RESOURCES

Various texts for shared and guided reading.

WHAT TO DO

Draw the children's attention to punctuation marks during shared and guided reading.

Ask the children why the marks might be there.

VARIATION

The children can be asked to consider punctuation in environmental print.

SPEECH BUBBLES

Children will use speech bubbles to learn about speech marks.

RESOURCES

Comic books, paper and coloured pencils, and whiteboard.

WHAT TO DO

Draw the children's attention to the speech bubbles in their comic books.

Give them the opportunity to draw up to six pictures telling their favourite story. They should write a sentence or two under each picture, but not dialogue.

Ask them to add speech bubbles.

As a whole class or group, take one or two of the children's pictures and write them out as texts, showing how the speech bubbles are written down as direct speech.

Some children will be able to then go on and translate their pictures and speech bubbles into written text.

VARIATION

The children can translate a short piece of narrative with dialogue into a comic strip.

REFERENCES

Bunting, R. (1997) *Teaching about Language in the Primary Years*. London: David Fulton.

Hall, N. (1996) 'Learning about punctuation: an introduction and overview', in N. Hall and A. Robinson (eds), *Learning about Punctuation*. Clevedon: Multilingual Matters.

Kelly, A. (2003) 'Transcription: spelling, punctuation and handwriting', in J. Graham and A. Kelly (eds), *Writing under Control* (2nd edition). Chiswick: David Fulton.

Waugh, D. and Jolliffe, W. (2017) *English 5–11: A Guide for Teachers*. London: Routledge.

FURTHER READING

Crystal, D. (2003) *The Cambridge Encyclopaedia of the English Language* (2nd edition). Cambridge: Cambridge University Press.

Crystal, D. (2005) *How Language Works*. London: Penguin.

Truss, L. (2009) *Eats, Shoots & Leaves: The Zero Tolerance Approach to Punctuation*. London: Profile Books.

Waugh, D., Warner, C. and Waugh, R. (2019) *Teaching Grammar, Punctuation and Spelling in Primary Schools* (3rd edition). London: SAGE.

USEFUL WEBSITES

For useful activities related to punctuation, see **www.schoolslinks.co.uk/GrammarForWriting.pdf**

For simple guidance on using punctuation marks, see **www.lexico.com/en/grammar/punctuation**

27

APOSTROPHES

WHAT DO I NEED TO KNOW?

Was there ever a punctuation mark more problematic than the use of the apostrophe? So simple, yet so misunderstood and misused! It is omitted when it should be used and inserted when it should not be used. We are all familiar with the ubiquitous examples of the greengrocers' apostrophe, as in 'potato's', 'carrot's' and 'tomato's', and the tendency of many people to use the apostrophe whenever a word ends in an 's'.

It really is quite simple. The apostrophe has two functions: to mark omission and to mark possession.

It marks omission (something is missing) as, for example, in the contractions 'can't', 'haven't', 'wouldn't' and 'who's', where the apostrophe is used in place of the missing letters. The apostrophe, used in this way, is found mainly in informal writing or in dialogue:

I can't come to meet you today, but I'll phone you later.

Where the apostrophe is used to mark possession, it is used differently to indicate singular and plural possession. In 'The boy's shoes', the shoes belong to one boy (singular). The apostrophe comes before the 's'. In 'The boys' shoes', the shoes belong to more than one boy (plural). The apostrophe comes after the 's'.

Where the plural of a noun is irregular – it is not made plural by the addition of an 's' (e.g. the plural of 'child' is 'children', the plural of 'man' is 'men') – the apostrophe comes after the 'n' and before the 's':

The children's performance was amazing.

The men's shirts are on the middle shelf.

Some possessive pronouns do not have an apostrophe. These are 'ours', 'yours', 'hers', 'theirs' and 'its'.

It is a common error to use the apostrophe with the possessive pronoun 'its'. The possessive of 'it' was originally 'it's' before being dropped at the beginning of the nineteenth century, and it is now only used as a contraction 'it's' for 'it is' or 'it has':

It's time for school.

The dog wagged its tail.

The only possessive pronoun to have an apostrophe is 'one's'. This is extended to 'someone's', 'everyone's' and 'no one's':

Is this someone's coat?

Everyone's drinks are on the table.

Some words end in 's', and when you want to indicate ownership an apostrophe and a second 's' are added to make it possessive, or you can put an apostrophe after the final 's':

This is James's bike. *Or* This is James' bike.

Jean Rhys's novels are wonderful. *Or* Jean Rhys' novels are wonderful.

In your own writing, it is important to be consistent in your usage.

The apostrophe is also commonly used in abbreviations of anglicised versions of Irish names (e.g. O'Connor, O'Neil, O'Brien), where the 'O' is short for 'of' (i.e. the person is the son of Connor, Neil or Brien).

An apostrophe is also used when writing time (e.g. 'ten o'clock'), where the 'o' is an abbreviation of 'of the' (i.e. 'ten of the clock').

It also indicates omission of figures in dates:

The summer of '93.

The apostrophe is used by writers to convey accent or dialect in the dialogue of a character. Charles Dickens, Thomas Hardy, George Bernard Shaw, Mark Twain, D.H. Lawrence and Emily Bronte are among the many writers to do so.

Frequent misuses of the apostrophe occur in the abbreviation, to their initials, of plural words. We have all seen the following:

CD's rather than CDs

MP's rather than MPs

MOT's rather than MOTs

WHAT IS IT USEFUL TO KNOW?

English is a Germanic language developed from the speech of the Angles, Saxons and Jutes – Germanic tribes who invaded England from northern Germany and southern Denmark in the fifth century.

As in modern German, old forms of English used a genitive case ending to show possession – normally '-es'. When Chaucer wrote his *Canterbury Tales* in the fourteenth century, one of the tales was 'Knyghtes Tale'. In modern varieties of English, the 'e' is missing. The old '-es' possessive form is not used so we use an apostrophe when letters are missing. 'The Knyghtes Tale' is now 'The Knight's Tale'.

The apostrophe was introduced into English from French in the sixteenth century and has had a long and confused history in attitudes and practice. Many large banks and businesses have dropped the apostrophe from their names (e.g. Barclays, Lloyds, Boots, Harrods and recently Waterstones – ironically a chain of bookshops), while other equally large businesses (e.g. Sainsbury's, McDonald's) have not done so. It is not surprising that many people feel unsure about the correct use and add an apostrophe before anything that ends in an 's'. The 'scattergun' approach means we see misplaced apostrophes everywhere.

The apostrophe is the only punctuation mark that arouses such strong feeling in people that there was even, until recently, an Apostrophe Protection Society (**www.apostrophe.org.uk**) started in Boston, Lincolnshire in 2001. It was run by a father and son who, when they spotted an incorrect use of the apostrophe by businesses, wrote to the company and suggested they may like to apply the correct usage. Although the founder has now retired from active involvement, the website is still up and running. Other people want to abolish the apostrophe, and an organisation called Kill the Apostrophe is dedicated to this (**www.killtheapostrophe.com**). It is true that the apostrophe, particularly for possession, could be abolished with little loss of meaning. The context is usually sufficient to indicate what is meant.

There is great inconsistency in the use of the apostrophe in British place names. Walk around any village, town or city and you will see evidence of this. You will see St Mary's Place and St Marys Place, King's Road and Kings Road. There is King's Lynn in Norfolk but Kings Langley in Hertfordshire.

When, in 2009, the city of Birmingham decided to lose the possessive apostrophe from signs, St Paul's Square became St Pauls Square. Supporters of the apostrophe started painting the apostrophe back on the signs at night.

The use of apostrophes in street names caused debate within Devon County Council and beyond (see **www.bbc.co.uk/news/uk-england-devon-21795179** and **www.bbc.co.uk/news/uk-england-devon-21835017**).

Next time you are out in and around your own locality, pay attention and see how the place names appear on signs.

KEY KNOWLEDGE SUMMARY

The apostrophe is a punctuation mark that is used to show possession or form contractions. An apostrophe should be used before an 's' if a noun is singular (e.g. 'the boy's book'). If the noun is plural, then the apostrophe should be added after the 's' (e.g. 'the girls' game').

When two words are combined to make a contraction, letters are removed and should be replaced by an apostrophe (e.g. 'they are' becomes 'they're' and 'he is' becomes 'he's').

IN THE CLASSROOM

Children need to know that apostrophes are used to show possession and also for contraction. They will learn simple basic rules but also some of the rules that apply only in certain circumstances. As with many adults, children will use apostrophes whenever there is an 's' at the end of a word. Particularly problematic is the apostrophe that indicates possession. It is important that there is a lot of discussion about the use of the apostrophe.

The basic rules that children will be taught are the following.

POSSESSION

If a noun is singular, the apostrophe goes before the 's' to show possession (e.g. 'the girl's hats'). This is an alternative way of writing 'the hats of the girl'. Do not be confused by the fact that there are a number of hats; it is the girl we are concerned with.

If the noun is plural and ends in an 's', then the apostrophe goes after the 's' (e.g. 'the girls' hats'). This is an alternative to writing 'the hats of the girls'.

All fairly straightforward. Problems usually arise when the plural of the noun does not end in 's'. Examples of these include 'men', 'children', 'sheep', 'teeth', 'feet' and so on. In these cases, the apostrophe comes before the 's' as in 'the men's coats', an alternative way of writing 'the coats belonging to the men'.

When a proper noun ends in an 's', you have a choice as to where to put the apostrophe, usually based on how it sounds. For example, the Newcastle United football stadium could be 'St James' Park' or 'St James's Park', but is usually 'St James' Park', while Exeter City, whose ground has the same name, sometimes miss out the apostrophe altogether!

The other rule to remember is that possessive pronouns do not have apostrophes (e.g. 'its', 'hers', 'yours', 'ours', 'theirs'). The only exception to this is 'one's'.

CONTRACTION

The other use of the apostrophe is to indicate omitted letters when a verb is contracted (e.g. 'he has' becomes 'he's', 'I am' becomes 'I'm', 'they have' becomes 'they've').

The children will learn that in more formal writing, the full form of the words is usually used.

You will see from the 'What is it useful to know?' section of this chapter that the teaching of the apostrophe is not going to be enhanced by looking around the environment. Perhaps when children become more experienced users of the apostrophe, they can go around the shops suggesting one or two changes.

Hall (2001) describes how an understanding of punctuation (and this would include the use of the apostrophe) comes when the child recognises that learning to read and write is meaningful. He goes on to say that notices around the classroom should be correctly punctuated and discussed with the children:

If there is an ethos in a classroom in which talk about learning is a real presence, and if children are curious about punctuation, then talk about punctuation will become part of the writing process.

(p151)

Because the apostrophe has two very different purposes, children need to be introduced to its use gradually, one use at a time.

The National Curriculum (DfE, 2013) requires pupils to learn the possessive apostrophe (singular) in Year 2 (6- to 7-year-olds). In this same year group, children should be taught how the apostrophe can be used for contractions (DfE, 2013, p57). As suggested earlier, the two functions should be taught separately. *Grammar for Writing* suggests an activity in which the children are presented with a short text in which some of the apostrophes are missing or in the wrong place (National Literacy Strategy, 2000). It is suggested that only apostrophes showing possession are used in the first exercise and then contraction when the exercise is repeated. This is one way of introducing the functions of apostrophes one at a time.

In Years 3 and 4, the National Curriculum requires that 'pupils should be taught to place the possessive apostrophe accurately in words with regular plurals … and in words with irregular plurals' (DfE, 2013, p37).

The most common confusion is between 'it's' as a contraction as in 'it's raining today' and 'its' as a possessive pronoun as in 'the parrot shook its feathers'. In the classroom activities section of this chapter, one of the activities, 'Sorting Apostrophes', addresses this to some extent, but discussion is essential.

CLASSROOM ACTIVITIES

PICTURING APOSTROPHES

Children will demonstrate their understanding of the possessive apostrophe by drawing accurate pictures.

RESOURCES

Paper and coloured pencils or paints.

WHAT TO DO

Ask the children to draw the following pictures to include the characters:

- the girl's cats;
- the girls' cats;
- the pirate's treasure; and
- the pirates' treasure.

SORTING APOSTROPHES

Children will show that they can differentiate between apostrophes for possession and apostrophes for contraction.

RESOURCES

Books, pencils and paper, and sheets with two columns, one headed 'P' for 'possession' and the other headed 'C' for contraction.

WHAT TO DO

Present the children with short texts and ask them to identify the words with apostrophes.

Ask them to write the words in the correct columns to demonstrate they understand the function of the apostrophe in each word.

USING APOSTROPHES

Children will apply their knowledge of using the apostrophe for contraction by creating their own sentences.

RESOURCES

Worksheet and pencils and paper.

WHAT TO DO

Make a worksheet for the children to complete.

Create a sentence for each of these words:

isn't   *shan't*   *it'll*   *mustn't*   *we've*

REFERENCES

DfE (2013) *The National Curriculum*. London: DfE.

Hall (2001) 'Developing understanding of punctuation with young writers and readers', in J. Evans (ed.), *The Writing Classroom*. London: David Fulton.

National Literacy Strategy (2000) *Grammar for Writing*. Available at: www.schoolslinks.co.uk/GrammarForWriting.pdf (accessed 13 October 2019).

FURTHER READING

Crystal, D. (2005) *How Language Works*. London: Penguin.

Morrison, T. (1987) *Beloved*. London: Chatto & Windus.

Truss, L. (2003) *Eats, Shoots & Leaves: The Zero Tolerance Approach to Punctuation*. London: Profile Books.

Waugh, D., Warner, C. and Waugh, R. (2019) *Teaching Grammar, Spelling and Punctuation in Primary Schools* (3rd edition). London: SAGE.

USEFUL WEBSITES

For the Apostrophe Protection Society's website, see **www.apostrophe.org.uk**

For simple guidance on using apostrophes, see **www.dreaded-apostrophe.com**

For a copy of the poem 'Apostrophe' by Roger McGough, see **iarumac.com/journal/twould-be-nice-to-be-an-apostrophe/**

28

BRINGING IT ALL TOGETHER

WHAT DO I NEED TO KNOW?

It is important that within text, there is consistency. This is achieved through cohesion and lack of ambiguity.

COHESION

Medwell et al. (2017) succinctly describe cohesion:

> *Cohesion in a story is the linking and the consistency of time and place and characters. Cohesion in a section of text is the linking of paragraphs both in content and in grammatical interdependence. Cohesion in a paragraph refers to the way that sentences interrelate … Cohesion in a sentence is achieved through such grammatical matters as consistency of noun/verb match, noun/pronoun match and verb tense.*
>
> (p201)

Cohesion is a crucial aspect of good writing, and it is the writer's job to make it clear to the reader how various parts of a text are connected. The parts of the text need to be related in meaningful ways to each other. The connections can be made by the two main types of cohesion: grammatical or lexical.

An example of grammatical cohesion is the use of pronouns. For example:

> The boy stole the bike and then he ran away. *('he' refers to 'The boy')*

> Sarah took the orange and ate it. *('it' refers to the 'orange')*

Lexical cohesion is achieved through the meanings of words the writer chooses rather than grammatical structure. Lexical cohesion includes repetition. In repetition, either words or phrases are directly repeated or synonyms (related words with similar meaning) are used. The straightforward repetition of a word has a cohesive effect because it creates a link between different sentences:

> *I have some great news to tell you. I know it is news you have all been waiting to hear.*

In this example, the repetition of the word 'news' has a cohesive effect.

AMBIGUITY

Ambiguity might occur when there are two or more meanings of a single word, phrase or sentence, leading to possible confusion. Ambiguity may sometimes be deliberate, but it is usually better to avoid it. Ambiguity in a single word is called lexical ambiguity. For example:

wave – to move the hand to and fro in greeting.

wave – one of a series of ridges or undulations that moves across a body of liquid, especially the sea.

Ambiguity in a sentence or clause is called structural ambiguity. For example:

This morning I ate an apple in my pyjamas. *(Was the apple wearing my pyjamas? Was I wearing my pyjamas when I ate the apple?)*

The sentence can be written clearly and without ambiguity:

This morning, in my pyjamas, I ate an apple.

WHAT IS IT USEFUL TO KNOW?

Intentional ambiguity, and sometimes unintentional ambiguity, can be seen in newspaper headlines. There are many examples – here are a few:

DRUNK GETS NINE MONTHS IN A VIOLIN CASE

LOCAL MAN FINDS PICASSO DRAWING IN SHED

MILK DRINKERS ARE TURNING TO POWDER

TEACHER STRIKES IDLE KIDS

KEY KNOWLEDGE SUMMARY

There should be consistency within a text so that a reader can make sense of the text. To be consistent, the writing should be cohesive and lack ambiguity. Cohesion in a sentence is achieved through ensuring that nouns and verbs agree, that nouns and pronouns match, and that tense is consistent. Where one word can have different meanings, it is important that the intended meaning is made clear and ambiguity avoided.

IN THE CLASSROOM

CONSISTENCY

The National Curriculum requires that children should be able to 'evaluate and edit by … ensuring the consistent and correct tense throughout a piece of writing [and] ensuring correct subject and verb agreement when using singular and plural' (DfE, 2013, p47).

Pupils, in their writing, often drift between tenses. For example:

> *It is a really hot day and I decided to go to the beach. I am very excited about this. I packed lots of snacks to keep me going as well as my bathing costume.*

You will see that sometimes the present tense has been used and sometimes the past tense. Of course, children can be given examples of written texts and asked to check the verb tenses to make the writing consistent.

However, the use of response partners can be more effective. Children reading their stories to each other often draw attention to inconsistencies that are missed when reading their own writing.

Similarly, children often find it difficult to sustain the same person when writing: they begin in the first person and then move into third, and vice versa. For example, a pupil might write:

> *I was dreading my first day going to work in the mill. I was only 10 and I knew it was going to be a long, hard day. She set off with her sister who had been working there for the past year.*

The child had been asked to write in the first person about working in Victorian times. She had started off in the first person but then reverted to third, which would be the way she usually wrote a report. One way of concentrating the children's minds to write consistently in the first person is to write in role during and following a drama activity.

COHESION AND COHESIVE DEVICES

Medwell et al. (2017) refer to cohesion as 'the linguistic glue that makes part of a text stick together' (p173).

In their writing, children need to organise the text so that features of cohesion are used. They should be made aware that it is important that the reader knows what is being referred to and can make sense of what is written. The National Curriculum requires that upper primary children should be taught to use 'a wide range of devices to build cohesion within and across paragraphs' (DfE, 2013, p47).

In developing cohesive strategies with children, it is important that discussion of texts takes place and that children draw on their own reading and spoken language to ensure cohesion. The substitution of personal pronouns for nouns is widely used in writing to replace the subject or the object of the sentence. Substitutions that refer to other parts of the text are perhaps the easiest cohesive devices to introduce to children. So, for example, if the class reads together a text such as the following, the children will be asked to offer alternative words to make the text less cumbersome:

> *Peter and Emily decided to have a picnic in the garden. Peter and Emily raided the fridge and found cheese, bread and juice. Peter and Emily took their cheese, bread and juice outside and put it on plates on a rug.*

The paragraph above is grammatically correct but reads very awkwardly. In the second and third sentences, 'Peter and Emily' can be replaced by the pronoun 'they'. In the third sentence, 'cheese, bread and juice' can be replaced by 'food' or 'picnic'.

These substitutions refer back to earlier sentences in the paragraph to ensure full meaning of the text. The paragraph with substitutions reads less awkwardly but at the same time remains cohesive.

Conjunctions are also important cohesive devices. An example of this is 'We must have breakfast before we go to school'. The conjunction 'before' makes the timing clear and gives the text cohesion.

AMBIGUITY

Children may like to see the well-known *Two Ronnies* 'Fork Handles'/'Four Candles' sketch, where lexical ambiguity has been used to very comical effect (see **www.youtube.com/watch?v=Cz2-ukrd2VQ**).

However, in normal written text ambiguity is to be avoided.

Different non-fiction genres use different cohesive devices. The following table has been taken from the National Strategies (DCSF, 2008). The final column gives the cohesive devices that are often used when writing a particular genre.

NON-FICTION TEXT TYPES AND COHESIVE DEVICES		
TEXT TYPE	**PURPOSE**	**COHESIVE DEVICES**
Discussion	To present a reasoned and balanced overview of an issue or controversial topic. Usually aims to provide two or more different views on an issue, each with elaborations, evidence and/ or examples.	Uses connectives, e.g. *for example, therefore, however.*
Explanatory	To explain how or why, e.g. to explain the processes involved in natural/social phenomena or to explain why something is the way it is.	Use of temporal connectives, e.g. *first, then, after that, finally.* Use of causal connectives, e.g. *so, because of this.*
Instructional/ procedural	Like all text types, variants of instructions occur and they can be combined with other text types. They may be visual only (e.g. a series of diagrams with an image for each step in the process) or a combination of words and images. Instructions and procedural texts are found in all areas of the curriculum and include rules for games, recipes, instructions for making something and directions.	Use of imperative verbs (commands), e.g. <u>Cut</u> the card, <u>Paint</u> your design. Instructions may include negative commands, e.g. *Do not use any glue at this stage.*
Persuasion	To argue a case from a particular point of view and to encourage the reader/listener towards the same way of seeing things.	Uses logical rather than temporal connectives, e.g. *This proves that, So it's clear, Therefore.*

(Continued)

(Continued)

NON-FICTION TEXT TYPES AND COHESIVE DEVICES		
TEXT TYPE	**PURPOSE**	**COHESIVE DEVICES**
Non-chronological reports	To provide detailed information about the way things are or were. To help readers/listeners understand what is being described by organising or categorising information.	Uses the language of comparison and contrast, e.g. *Polar bears are the biggest carnivores of all. They hibernate, just like other bears. A polar bear's nose is as black as a piece of coal.*
Recounts	The primary purpose of recounts is to retell events. Their most common intentions are to inform and/or entertain.	Events being recounted have a chronological order so temporal connectives are common, e.g. *then, next, first, afterwards, just before that, at last, meanwhile.*

These cohesive devices can be presented to children as writing frames to support their writing of specific genres. For example, the following writing frame can be given to children to support their writing of a recount, perhaps of a recent visit. Temporal connectives are used as the cohesive devices.

A Visit to the Coast

First of all, we …

Then we …

After that, it was …

In the meantime, we …

Finally, we …

As always when using writing frames, it is important that children move on to independent writing as quickly as possible, having learned how to plan for a particular text type.

CLASSROOM ACTIVITIES

CONSISTENCY OF PERSON

Children will write consistently in the first person by writing in role.

RESOURCES

Paper and pens, and a copy of 'The Pied Piper of Hamelin' by Robert Browning.

WHAT TO DO

The children will have read 'The Pied Piper of Hamelin'.

The children are seated. The teacher, in role, enters the room.

The teacher says:

You know I am the mayor of Hamelin. I am here to listen to your complaints about the rats in the town. I am pleased that, as residents of Hamelin, you have found the time to come and speak with me. Now, tell me what has been going on.

The teacher encourages the children (residents) to voice their concerns.

The teacher then says:

It's important that I have all of these examples in writing so that I can go to the health and safety committee. It must be your experiences that you write about, so I would expect everything to be written in the first person.

CREATING A COHESIVE TEXT

Children will reorganise sentences into a cohesive text, learning that temporal connectives are used as cohesive devices when the narrative is chronological. They will also learn that a sentence containing a pronoun should refer back to a previous sentence containing a noun.

RESOURCES

Pieces of laminated card. Each of the following sentences should be written on separate pieces of card:

Once upon a time, there were three bears: daddy bear, mummy bear and baby bear.

They were going to have breakfast, but their porridge was too hot.

They decided to go for a walk.

In the meantime, Goldilocks, who had been walking in the woods, came to the bears' house.

She came into the house and smelled the porridge.

WHAT TO DO

The children will be asked to put the strips in the correct order. The resulting story should be discussed to ensure it is chronologically correct and that pronouns are referring back to the appropriate previous sentence.

RECOGNISING AMBIGUITY

Children will recognise ambiguity in newspaper headlines.

RESOURCES

Paper and coloured pencils, and whiteboard.

WHAT TO DO

The teacher shows the children the following headlines and asks them to comment on the two possible meanings of the headlines:

CHEF THROWS HIS HEART INTO HELPING FEED NEEDY

KIDS MAKE NUTRITIOUS SNACKS

RED TAPE HOLDS UP NEW BRIDGES

STOLEN PAINTING FOUND BY TREE

The children are then asked to choose one headline and draw the two possible meanings.

REFERENCES

DCSF (2008) *The National Strategies*. London: DCSF.

DfE (2013) *The National Curriculum*. London: DfE.

Medwell, J. and Wray, D. with Moore, G. and Griffiths, V. (2007) *Primary English, Knowledge and Understanding* (8th edition). Exeter: Learning Matters.

FURTHER READING

Waugh, D., Warner, C. and Waugh, R. (2019) *Teaching Grammar, Punctuation and Spelling in Primary Schools* (3rd edition). London: SAGE.

29

THE GRAMMAR, PUNCTUATION AND SPELLING TEST

WHAT DO I NEED TO KNOW?

The Key Stage 2 grammar, punctuation and spelling test was introduced in 2013 as part of the end of Key Stage assessments. It was intended to:

- ensure that children leave primary school confident in spelling, punctuation and grammar; and

- encourage schools to place more emphasis on the teaching of these skills than before.

The test was updated in 2016 to bring it into line with the National Curriculum (DfE, 2013), and was made more challenging.

It assesses elements of the programme of study for English in the current National Curriculum, particularly the following:

- word classes;

- functions of sentences;

- combining words, phrases and clauses;

- verb forms, tenses and consistency;

- vocabulary, particularly adding affixes, synonyms and antonyms;

- Standard English and levels of formality;

- punctuation; and

- spelling.

The programme of study includes a significant level of detail in terms of spelling (outlined in DfE, 2013, Appendix 1) and vocabulary, grammar and punctuation (outlined in DfE, 2013, Appendix 2). The test covers aspects encountered in lower as well as upper Key Stage 2.

Children take two papers:

- *Paper 1.* This paper contains 50 questions on grammar, vocabulary and punctuation, combining multiple-choice questions and short-answer questions, and takes 45 minutes.

- *Paper 2.* This is the spelling paper and takes about 15 minutes. There are 20 words to spell; children hear a sentence that includes the target word read aloud, and they fill in the missing word in the sentence in their answer booklets.

WHAT IS IT USEFUL TO KNOW?

TERMINOLOGY

Terminology is seen as being important because it gives children the technical vocabulary to discuss their own reading, writing and oral language. Some of the questions can be answered without knowledge of terminology, using common sense and 'what fits', but others cannot be answered without knowledge of terminology such as 'simple past tense', 'relative clause', 'modal verb', 'noun phrase', 'passive', 'coordinating conjunction', 'subordinate clause', 'antonym', 'Standard English', 'colon' and 'relative pronoun'. Roughly a third of the questions are on punctuation, with six on vocabulary and the rest grammar. Children who use Standard English at home may be at an advantage when identifying standard forms, as these will sound right to them in a way they will not to children who speak another dialect.

TEST SCORES

The 'pass mark' for the test may vary from year to year: in 2016, it was 43 out of 70; in 2018, 38 out of 70; and in 2018 and 2019, 36 out of 70. The raw score is converted to a scaled score in which 100 represents attainment of the expected standard.

THE KEY STAGE 1 TEST

The Key Stage 1 grammar, punctuation and spelling test is optional. It consists of two papers:

- *Paper 1: spelling.* As with the Key Stage 2 paper, children have an answer booklet with 20 sentences, in each of which the target word is missing. The teacher reads out the complete sentence and children fill in the target word.

- *Paper 2: grammar and punctuation.* There were 20 questions in 2018. Of these, six related to punctuation, five to word classes, three to verb tenses and consistency, two to vocabulary (adding affixes), two to functions of sentences, and two to using conjunctions to combine words, phrases and clauses. To be able to answer all the questions successfully, children would need to know the terminology 'noun', 'adjective', 'verb', 'adverb', 'statement', 'command', 'exclamation', 'past tense', 'present tense', 'apostrophe' and 'comma'.

The 2018 pass mark was 24 out of 40.

KEY KNOWLEDGE SUMMARY

WHAT IS THE GRAMMAR, PUNCTUATION AND SPELLING TEST?

It is one of the end of key stage tests (SATs), and is based on the content of the National Curriculum English programme of study. There are two papers, one covering grammar and punctuation and one for spelling. The Key Stage 1 test is optional for schools.

IN THE CLASSROOM

DOES EVERY PUPIL HAVE TO TAKE THE TEST?

Pupils do not take the test if they have not completed the relevant programme of study, or are working below the overall standard (i.e. unable to answer the easiest questions), or are working at the standard but cannot participate even when using suitable access arrangements (provided for children with specific needs).

Children in the early stages of learning English as an additional language may not need to take the test.

Children with dyslexia or other specific learning difficulties may be given a reader for the test, at the school's discretion.

Children with dyspraxia or other motor difficulties may be given a scribe.

Children with a hearing impairment who are unable to access the spelling test (e.g. by using British Sign Language or lip-reading) are given compensatory marks.

CAN SCHOOLS PREPARE CHILDREN FOR THE TEST?

It is difficult to 'teach to the test' when the test is of knowledge about language and the spelling system. The relevant skills and understanding need to be developed over time, and only some aspects of punctuation and test techniques are likely to be improved with a last-minute revision programme.

An understanding of grammar – the way words are put together to build phrases, clauses, sentences and texts – develops through exploration and discussion of real texts, whether these are ones that pupils are reading or ones they are writing. Children are much more likely to understand and remember if they are interested in what they are learning and see its relevance. Decontextualised exercises, of the 'underline the adverbs in these sentences' type, are unlikely to inspire, and often the superficial knowledge acquired does not transfer to the analysis of real language. For example, children may think that adverbs always end with '-ly', and therefore identify 'quickly' as an adverb but not 'fast'. The 2019 test had a question aimed at this misconception, which asked children to pick out the adverb from 'lovely', 'wobbly', 'neatly' and 'curly'.

GETTING TO GRIPS WITH TERMINOLOGY

Terminology is best learned in three phases:

PHASE 1: FAMILIARISATION

The teacher uses the terminology in context, so children hear it and begin to develop an understanding of what it means.

For example, in guided reading, the teacher says:

> *I wonder why the author has used those two adjectives, 'grey' and 'faint'?*

Or in shared writing, the teacher says:

> *I think I'll start the sentence with my adverb: 'Carefully, he edged along the ledge'.*

Children may need to hear terminology used in this way, accurately and confidently, many times, before they are ready to use it themselves.

PHASE 2: TEACHING

A clear explanation of the term being taught is given (the 2014 programme of study glossary provides a useful starting point), along with a number of examples (DfE, 2013). Children might then look for their own examples in a shared text or their own reading book or writing.

PHASE 3: APPLICATION

Children spontaneously use the terminology when talking about texts, demonstrating their understanding of it.

PREPARING CHILDREN FOR THE TEST

Preparation for the test is likely to be a combination of revision of some aspects of subject knowledge and test techniques.

SUBJECT KNOWLEDGE

Children are more likely to remember subject knowledge if they engage with it actively, and in regular short bursts. To revise word classes, for example, children could text-mark passages, underlining or highlighting different word classes in different colours.

TEST TECHNIQUE

Despite many reminders, pupils taking tests often make basic mistakes such as spending too long on a question they do not understand and then rushing others, or not reading the questions properly, or leaving a multiple-choice question blank rather than guessing.

Rather than keep reminding children of the dos and don'ts of tests, put the children in charge by asking them, after taking a practice test, to reflect on any mistakes they made and difficulties they had, to draw up their own list of reminders and tips. These can be shared, and if anything important has been omitted it can be added. At a later date, children can play 'top tip tennis' in pairs, taking turns to give a tip until no more can be remembered.

CLASSROOM ACTIVITIES

PUNCTUATION PUZZLE

RESOURCES

Copies of a text that uses a variety of punctuation marks, with each different punctuation mark replaced by a symbol such as a wingding (e.g. all the full stops replaced by ❖, all the apostrophes replaced by ♌).

WHAT TO DO

The children work in pairs to discover which punctuation mark each wingding represents. This task can be differentiated if necessary, with some texts including a wider range of punctuation marks, such as semicolons and dashes. When feeding back on their findings, the children should explain how they worked out the code, rather than simply what it was.

HUMAN SENTENCES

RESOURCES

Large word cards with a range of nouns, determiners, adjectives, verbs, adverbs, prepositions and conjunctions.

WHAT TO DO

A group of children hold up their cards to form a human sentence. Pick one card and ask which other children could replace it in the sentence. Only words of the same word class would fit.

Play the word substitution game – start with a human sentence, with the children holding the different words on cards. Distribute other word cards and see which words can replace which in the sentence. Only words of the same word class will fit.

REFERENCES

DfE (2013) *The National Curriculum*. London: DfE.

Standards and Testing Agency (2018) *Key Stage 1 Tests: 2018 English Grammar, Punctuation and Spelling Test Materials*. Available at: www.gov.uk/government/publications/key-stage-1-tests-2018-english-grammar-punctuation-and-spelling-test-materials (accessed 30 May 2019).

Standards and Testing Agency (2019) *Key Stage 2 Tests: 2019 English Grammar, Punctuation and Spelling Test Materials*. Available at: www.gov.uk/government/publications/key-stage-2-tests-2019-english-grammar-punctuation-and-spelling-test-materials (accessed 30 May 2019).

FURTHER READING

Corbett, P. (2004) *Jumpstart! Key Stage 2/3 Literacy Games*. London: David Fulton.

Medwell, J. (2012) *Primary English Knowledge and Understanding*. London: SAGE.

National Literacy Strategy (2000) *Grammar for Writing*. Available at: www.schoolslinks.co.uk/GrammarForWriting.pdf (accessed 13 October 2019).

Standards and Testing Agency (2019) *Information for Parents: 2019 National Curriculum Tests at the End of Key Stages 1 and 2*. Available at: www.gov.uk/government/publications/key-stage-1-and-2-national-curriculum-tests-information-for-parents/information-for-parents-2019-national-curriculum-tests-at-the-end-of-key-stages-1-and-2-text-only-version (accessed 30 May 2019).

Waugh, D., Warner, C. and Waugh, R. (2019) *Teaching Grammar, Punctuation and Spelling in Primary Schools* (3rd edition). London: SAGE.

INDEX